Always Seek God First

An
Alcoholic's
Journey to
GOD

Always Seek God First

An
Alcoholic's
Journey to
GOD

366 Daily Devotional Read

SAMI G.

Mill City Press

Mill City Press, Inc.
2301 Lucien Way #415
Maitland, FL 32751
407.339.4217
www.millcitypress.net

Unless otherwise indicated, Scripture quotations taken from the Holy Bible, New Living Translation (NLT). Copyright ©1996, 2004, 2007 by Tyndale House Foundation. Used by permission of Tyndale House Publishers, Inc.

Scripture quotations taken from the King James Version (KJV) – *public domain*.

Printed in the United States of America.

ISBN-13: 9781545642856

Table of Contents

Acknowledgments

I would like to give a huge thanks to my family and friends and fellow members. I am so grateful to God for every lesson, every joyful moment, and even every heartache, because with it there was growth and healing.

I would like to give a shout out to Watershed of Florida for the safe, friendly, caring staff. It was the beginning of my journey back to God and sobriety, so thank you.

Thank you Shaiann and Cain for believing in me and for your encouragement, and I quote, "Remember Grandma, don't get discouraged, if someone doesn't like it, just send it to someone else; keep trying." I love you both!

My husband, David: words cannot express the love between us. Your support has always been boundless and I thank you.

Jessica and Israel: thank you for your endless talks of God and the ten thousand questions answered!

Mother and Father, sisters and brother, it has been one hell of a good/bad/indifferent life. Thank you all for your continued support and love.

My daughter Tonya, there is always hope and serenity in sobriety. I love you.

A heart-felt thank you to Cindy, Sabrina, Chevelle and the team members behind the scenes for their hard work and dedication.

"For where you have envy and selfish ambition, there you find disorder and evil practice." James 3:16

Did you know none of us is immune to temptation? Looking back, I can see where I sinned. I can see where the beam in my mind became so narrow and unimportant that I picked up a drink after seven years of sobriety. I know what it feels like to become detached from my fellowship and have no defense against that first drink. I no longer made myself accountable to God, but wide open to Satan's tactics.

Introduction

It does not matter if we were a functional drunk, a fall down drunk, an angry drunk, or a pitiful drunk, because our results were always the same. We drank to become drunk, we passed out, and then began a brand-new day the exact same way. Our business suffered and our families suffered, but somehow, we just could not stop drinking on our own willpower. We had false pride, big egos, and short tempers.

Yet, there a came a day for us that we experienced a saving grace. We could not explain it, but we felt it, and shortly after joining our fellowship, we began to learn of our obsession and compulsion. The greatest explanation of our illness comes from a well-known physician of his time, Dr. William Duncan Silkworth, who was known as "the little doctor who loved drunks" and was named the "medical saint" of his time. In his practice, he treated well over forty thousand alcoholics, and it is known in the science of medicine of that time, alcoholism was a hopeless disease, but Dr. Silkworth was convinced of two things: First, "Alcoholism is not just a vice or habit. This is a compulsion; this is a pathological craving, this disease." Secondly, he says, "It is an obsession of the mind that condemns one to drink and an allergy of the body that condemns one to die." There is a third idea that probably followed upon Dr. Silkworth's experience with Bill Wilson that "unless (the alcoholic) can experience an entire psychic change, there is little hope of his recovery."

We need to be grateful to these men and woman who came before us, and for their guidance to finding a power greater than ourselves. I know for me, journaling along my journey to God brought me inspiration, and it has led me to a deep relationship with Him. Through God's Word, wisdom, guidance, and Holy Spirit, I have discovered "the void" to be filled. I come to share my experience, strength, and hope in that at least one other alcoholic will be saved today. After all, it is our motto: "one day at a time."

I believe another important part of recovery is keeping a journal. I love the fourth step because its intentions let us get it all down in black and white, so it is glaring at us to see. I need to see my words and reflect back to see where there is growth and where I am blocked from God. Maybe that's what prompted my book idea, because I can look back on my journey, and in the years 2008-2009, I see through my writings the downward spiral I took. Seven years of recovery gone with one drink. The next six years were a drunken blur. The last three years were a recovery once more, and a part of my healing process is in this manuscript.

If you're struggling, then you are struggling with the God idea. The Scriptures that God lead me to while writing this book told me my life story. My recovery depends upon the book of *Alcoholics Anonymous*, combined with God's words written in the other "big book", we have a recipe for a beautiful life.

Before we begin there are a few questions we need to ask ourselves throughout our sobriety: Am I open-minded? Am I willing? Am I honest enough to continue along a spiritual journey to remain sober? All of these questions need an answer; they need for us to make a decision: yes or no.

I pray that my words are useful and my story gives you strength. God put hope in your hands, use it. Please continue to read a verse a day and experience the healing journey God will bring you of your own. Journaling is good for the soul, so enjoy, go in peace, God bless, and have a slow recovery.

This is my story as I crossed the river of denial

I always dabbled in alcohol, with my first drunk experience when I was a young girl at a family party with relatives. There wasn't a consequence really, but I do remember it as clear as yesterday. I remembered that first high. Now, in hindsight, that is the exact high I was always searching for. It was the 60s and 70s—everybody partied; everybody drank! Thinking back, my basic necessities were always met. I was the youngest of four. I never went to bed hungry. I always had clothes on my back and shoes on my feet. There were family vacations. But, when I think back to that little girl growing up, I always remember there wasn't peace in her heart. I had a part of me that loved my family, but a bigger part of me that was amiss. I was mean and egotistical, even as a child. I often sat and wondered if there was something I missed as a little girl that I felt so disconnected as I grew. Later in life I found that answer: God.

I couldn't wait to grow up. I was never content with being who I was. I always looked in the mirror with such disgust, so I learned early on that the best highs made me feel less like a nobody. I always compared myself to others and I felt that I never measured up. My own soul was a lonely place to sit in day after day. My mind, will, and emotions did not play well with one another. In fact, there was so much torture and chaos that I had to shut them up, and alcohol and drugs were the solution.

Would life be different today if I was not an alcoholic? Would life make more sense today? Would it have been easier or more successful? Along my journey, I have pondered these questions many times. To this day, I still don't have the answers. Maybe because there is no answer for what could have been. I was a prisoner to my addiction early in life, because most days life just escaped me. I was different and I always felt alone—not lonely, just alone. It became easier to pop a pill, snort a line, drink some booze, smoke a joint. I just didn't care, so I became hurtful and hateful, so I drank some more.

My mind was always racing. Running from one thought to another. It was so dark and gloomy inside my head. I needed an escape and that's what I found in any substance that altered my mind. Sometimes I wish my story was different, but it is not. Choices were made, mistakes along the way. Lessons learned; maybe. I wish I had known the easier softer way, but they say we get there when we get there. However, today, as an alcoholic, I can say I have lived two lives: one drunk and one sober.

The seven deadly sins reared their ugliness early in life for me, and this is probably for the choices I made so young. The booze, then the drugs compounded every negative thought, but I believed at the time they made life better, happier, lighter. Alcohol lowered my inhibitions. It was my friend for a long time—a very long time. However, that one day came when that bottle turned into my greatest enemy. I became so blind to the fact that little by little my addictions were slowly stealing my soul while turning me into a liar, a cheat, and a thief. I was just a young child navigating through this world and I was confused, and baffled by the person I was becoming. Nobody understood me. I stood alone in the world. But I thought I was always in control, because my pride wouldn't have it any other way, but it was always a facade. I was a fake, a phony, and a greedy person who was never satisfied.

I absolutely loathed myself. I took my young life and made one choice after another with booze and drugs. I kept searching for something that I could not find: serenity. So I lived this life full of envy, jealousy, fear, lies, contempt, hatred—the list can go on and on. I did not realize as a young child how selfish my inner child was, and it remained that way far into adulthood. I still believed alcohol was the solution. It was the cure for my tormented mind.

Shame, guilt, and remorse took over my life. But the insanity of this is that I kept doing the same thing over and over and over again. The merry-go-round wouldn't stop; it wouldn't let me off. Suicide contemplation was always in the equation. Quite frankly, I was the undisciplined type. I always, always wanted more, while self-seeking and selfishly thinking what was in it for me. I was determined to learn life the hard way. I was a bully to others, skipping school, getting bad grades, being disrespectful to my elders because I knew everything. I was always self-sabotaging because I didn't care. You know that old saying, "I would shoot myself in my own foot to spite you"? Well, that was me.

I always opened the door to Satan, because I knew I wasn't worthy of God's love. So I drank to become drunk and then I drank some more. Some days I woke up and I was good with the world, and I would think less of myself, but most days I struggled. I've learned through the years that I must be careful, because emotions are fickle. It is almost like you cannot trust them. One moment they care, the next they don't. It is a roller coaster—up, down, forward, backward. Will it stop? Does it stop? I know one thing for sure: drinking only intensified the ride. It made it extremely unstable.

Besides alcohol, my true love is marijuana. This had me hook, line, and sinker! I was twelve years of age and it became a daily use. If I had to steal for my habit then that's exactly what I did. Life changed around that age. My siblings were gone, my parents were drifting apart, and I had such low self-esteem and extreme hatred for myself.

I remember one summer day I found my mother half-dead of an overdose. This changed something deep in my heart. I closed myself off. The friends I sought after were older and the ones my parents didn't approve of, but I couldn't care less. School became less important and my need for drugs and alcohol grew. I thought I was smart about my addictions because I hid it so well. I was in denial that I was heading for trouble, and because my friends were older, I just saw that they were worse off than myself.

Life went on into thirteen and fourteen. As more time went on, the more bitter I became. All I remember is that I hated life. I had plenty of friends, but I still felt that I stood alone. I had a young love relationship at fourteen, and one day found myself pregnant. I was so young, but I had to make a life-changing decision. The choice was to keep my child. The disappointment I caused my parents was horrifying, and a feeling of guilt over-whelmed me. I broke my parents' heart. They told me I ruined my life. This guilt stayed with me for a very long time. I wish I can say that this put a halt to my disease, however, it wasn't until I was four months pregnant that I put the drugs down. I was so naive, selfish, and full of fear. Although I was in a rela-tionship with my child's father, I was still very much alone and life went on.

I promised myself I was going to be a good mom. When the doctor put that beautiful, healthy baby girl in my arms, I convinced myself that she would save my life, and I would never touch another drink or drug. And I brought this child, this gift from God, home to play house with and for a month I was great, but unfortunately, I found myself alone again and that promise to myself to never drink again was broken. Drugs and alcohol became a part of my life again and many, many years would pass by. I grew up with my daughter doing what I thought was the best I could do, but I left her with family as often as I could. I put her in harm's way many times when I was a dealer of cocaine and marijuana and had strangers coming in and out of our home. I taught her to keep secrets of what Mom and Dad were doing at home, and I spent my time alone with my daughter taking shots of whiskey and brandy, smoking pot, popping pain killers, and snorting lines.

My friends were off to high school to live their lives and figure out what their next move will be for their future. Although I had quit school in eighth grade, I did manage to make it back to two years of continued education and earned my high school diploma. Some college was within my years, but I could never keep it together long enough to complete my degree. I lost my soul somewhere and days turned into nights which turned into weeks and then years. Alcohol was always there and drug choices changed throughout the years. My addictions were silent killers and I was in extreme denial.

I did marry my daughter's father, but of course it was puppy love and volatile. There were good times, but never enough, because of alcohol, drugs, and extramarital affairs. Many years were wasted with bitterness, resentments, hostile thoughts, and anger. Nothing felt good. My mind was just always disturbed. Years went by and I divorced. I ran far away with a geographical change. I am now in a new relationship and feeling happy, for now. There were still drugs and alcohol, but it seemed less of a problem and life went on. Everything seemed good through the honeymoon stage!

I tread lightly when I write about the next several years. They are painful and humiliating. Guilt, shame, and remorse started taking over my life again. My daughter became a hostage throughout my life. She saw things she shouldn't, experienced things in my world that damaged her. I was in such denial of my own disease. I was controlling and demanding and I started to hate life all over again. Shame on me because I brought my daughter into the world of drugs and alcohol. At twelve I was smoking pot with her and by sixteen we were sharing some drinks, and by seventeen we would exchange pills. In my sick mind, I was doing the right thing. I convinced myself she was safer doing all these things at home where she would be safe, as opposed to doing them in the outside world. However, eventually her friends became my friends, her dealers became my dealers, and life went on, painfully. My daughter lost many friends in death to this disease, and you would think that would have opened both of our eyes, but it didn't. We mourned them and went on with our addictions and life as usual.

I was on the brink of losing everything I built because of the booze. My husband and I had to take a good look at our lives, because it was being destroyed by our addictions. Then there came a day, it was Fourth of July weekend, a true miracle happened and God shed His grace on my husband. He gave him a moment of clarity. He gave him courage and strength to make a change. He showed him the doors to Alcoholics Anonymous. I followed shortly thereafter, because I was in such denial of my own addictions. My ego told me I was better than everyone else and that I had no problem. It took some months to learn the twelve steps and the principles of honesty, hope, faith, courage, integrity, willingness, humility, brotherly love, justice, perseverance, spiritual awareness, and service would save my life and my husband's, but sadly not my daughter's. I tried to convince her of a spiritual way, but it went to the wayside, so I had to heal myself and pray and pray for her to find her way.

Slowly but surely, God started to do work in my life, in my family, in my home, and in my marriage. I did what was suggested. I didn't drink and I attended meetings, I raised my hand so people got to know me. I wasn't alone anymore, because finally I understood: I am an alcoholic. I got a sponsor and we worked through the steps with the Big Book. I got a home group and started doing service. I came to know my God on a personal level and realized He had been with me the whole time; it was me who abandoned Him. I had to die to my old self. I had to ask God to show me how to grow in the Holy Spirit and every day I prayed this prayer of mine:

> I cannot run my life anymore on my own will. I do not want to be self-absorbed any longer. I want to spread your love, kindness, and tolerance to others. I no longer need to live in my past. I give all my sorrows to you. Please aid me in spreading your good news to the next sick and suffering alcoholic. I know, from your word God, that I never have to be alone and drunk again, Amen.

It was difficult to get sober when my daughter was still active. The best suggestion I received early on was to stay firmly planted in the rooms, because I was finally living life on life's terms, and was able to be a better role model and mother. I was to put forth the work and continue to pray for my beautiful daughter.

In 2003, my first grandchild was born. Another true miracle from God, and things seemed to look up for my daughter. I thought, *what a saving grace; my most precious granddaughter*. I was able to love her completely because of sobriety. Being sober meant everything to me. This child was the apple of Mami and Papi's eye!

I began to learn to love myself. I could actually look in the mirror and see me, and love me. I humbled myself and I gave back what was so freely given to me. Years went by and my husband and I remained sober. In 2006, we celebrated a grandson into the world. My husband and I helped raise these two magnificent children. Maybe, in some way, God was allowing me to heal some part of me for being such a terrible mother. My life was not perfect, but pretty damn close. However, my daughter's started to fall apart once again. This insidious disease shows no mercy and does not discriminate.

One day, I started to get in my own way. I can look back now, in hindsight, and see the picture unfold. It was 2008 and I slowly but surely allowed my meetings to lose their priority. All of that stuff—the ego, the pride, the self-loathing—was seeping back into my soul. I couldn't seem to control the downward spiral that was happening. The worst part is that I no longer put God first and by 2009, the drinking began.

It is not exactly clear the day I put that bottle of vodka to my lips again. In fact, the next six years remain unclear. Something inside of me broke and my whole sober foundation came tumbling down. Satan was in full attack and I didn't have the will to fend him off because I had left God behind. I still ask myself *why, why, why did I pick up that drink*, but then I gently remind myself, *it is because I am an alcoholic*, and I was no longer communing with God, working my program, or helping another alcoholic. I couldn't give away any longer what I once had. So I had to accept it as it was; I chose to pick up that first drink and return back to the living gates of hell.

My husband relapsed around the same time and we were both on a path that led to everything being alcohol fueled. If you didn't drink as much as we did, we didn't have much use for you. Everything came second to our drinking. We were both functional for years until the alcohol started tearing us down, and the fighting returned once again. A part of me thanks God that through all our drinking days, we remained together, for when I fell, he picked me up, and when he fell, I was there to pick him up. Family close to us just looked on with sorrow, because there was nothing that anyone could do or say. Once again, I broke my parents' heart.

Year after year went by and we remained drunk. I was not only verbally abusive, but physically abusive. My husband had to explain away scratches and black eyes to fellow workers. Although I was an abusive wife, he never laid a hand on me except to defend himself. I was always so remorseful until the next morning's drink kicked in. I knew AA was the answer so I stayed far, far away from it. I was in bed with Satan again. Not even the doctors' warnings that my health was showing signs of disaster, because of the amount of alcohol I was consuming, could stop me.

By this time, it was summer 2012. I was employed and functioning, but soon working was in my way. I began drinking during lunch breaks. Alcohol consumed my life; my every thought; my every move, and two more years passed by with me in a drunken stupor. While my life was deteriorating, so was my daughter's, twelve hundred miles away. I received a phone call one day in late 2013 that she was in the hospital, on life support, and my grandchildren needed me. My husband and I promised each other that we would put the drink down for the sake of the children. We did try on our own will power, but the alcohol won. It was too strong to handle on our own, and Satan kept nipping at our heels, so the next six months, we were raising two children resentfully, and drunk.

In July 2014, I sent my grandchildren back to their mother. I knew in my heart that I shouldn't. I will always regret my decision, but I loved alcohol more than anything or anybody in my life. I was consumed with it and I started to isolate. I quit work and my drinking began early in the morning. At this point I was drinking around the clock. Shamefully, I had to tell my family not to tell me anything after 1:30 pm, because I couldn't remember a thing. I saw the toll that alcohol was taking on my husband. I knew we had to quit because we were killing ourselves, slowly.

My husband and I had relocated September 2014. This is where my isolation became a huge problem. At least before the move, I always tried to be presentable. I always tried to have a hot meal at the end of the day for my husband, however, that soon started to lose its appeal. I wasn't falling asleep anymore, for I was just passing out, and the blackouts even started to scare me. Delirium tremors were happening some nights and I would wake to think there were bugs surrounding me and climbing all over my body, but I kept on drinking.

One afternoon in December, my husband and I set out to have lunch with each other. It was about 1:30 in the afternoon. I know we ordered food, but of course the drinks kept flowing. My memory is hazy, but we left the bar around 6:00-7:00 that evening, and it was a rainy night. I convinced my husband to allow me to drive because I was the more sober one; lie. It is all a blur, but I totaled my husband's vehicle that night. I do remember it was in a well-lit neighborhood, but no one heard the crash. I remember the roads were slick and icy and I lost control of the car and it just kept spinning and spinning and finally we came to a stop after smashing into a parked vehicle. The driver's side and all the side windows blew out from the impact and I remember the fear that gripped me that I would be arrested. I just kept repeating to myself, "God, please get me out of here," while I was putting the truck between drive and reverse to get us free from the car I hit. To this day, we do not know where the crash took place. I lived in fear the next couple days expecting the police to knock on my door, because it was a hit and run. Thank God no one died that rainy night. The insanity is that we still drank and drove. My whole life was crumbling, and I knew the alcohol was driving me toward the brink of death. I didn't want to get drunk, but I did not want to give up the booze. I truly wanted to die, because at this point I was just existing. I had forgotten about the people who loved me and I didn't care that I was a wife, a daughter, a mother, a sister, a grandmother, an aunt, and a friend.

On Thursday, January 8, 2015, something happened. Something changed. I heard God's call. All I remember about that day is my daughter calling me, and me agreeing that I would go to rehab. But not that day, "No, no," I said, "on Sunday." So I spent the next three days in complete drunkenness. On Sunday morning, my daughter flew from her home to take me to the airport. My daughter, who was still sick and suffering herself, helping her mother on a plane, drunk and barely coherent— what shame. Being put in a taxi for the airport by my husband was scary; bitter, yet sweet. All that remained on my mind was to pray for my husband. We were both going to get well. That was our promise to each other. Could we keep that promise? Yes, we could!

I ran back into the arms of sobriety. It took me two to three days to get my feet planted back on the ground from detox. I knew the desperation to get back to a soundness of mind; I needed my sanity back; I needed my dignity back. I am twice gifted within AA and I once again found myself full of gratitude. God's grace saved me once again! When I returned from rehab, my husband kept the promise he made to me, because he said to me while I was getting into the taxi, "You go, get better, and then we can take care of me," and that day, February 4, 2015, when I returned back to him was his last drink. My husband and I started to rebuild our foundation in sobriety again; hallelujah!

I wasn't sure where life was going to take me in sobriety, but becoming a mother again to my two grandchildren six months into it wasn't exactly what I had in mind. Once again, I received a phone call that my grandchildren were in desperate need of rescue. In my prayers I asked God to reveal to me what I was supposed to do. I now had full custody of my two grand-children. I had put my daughter in God's care, because there was nothing more I could do for her, but pray and raise her children in a sober environment. During all this, a third grandchild was born. However, I became legal guardian to the two oldest, while my second grandson remained in the custody of his father. Sometimes when I sit all alone into the nighttime hours, I still feel so powerless. I wish I could fix the damage done to the beautiful souls of my grandchildren and my only daughter, but I have come to know that I cannot play God. My faith in our Lord gives me comfort in knowing it is His will, and I have to put all my trust and all my faith in Him. There are no guarantees in this life on Earth, because each day that dawns has troubles all of its own. It has been painful watching the ripple effect of these innocent children, knowing that I can only do my best, and it is frustrating feeling that my best is not good enough. However, I have learned that I am only responsible for the effort and not the outcome.

The Prayer of St. Francis is a powerful tool for me, because its meaning is deeply entrenched with enlightenment. In our twelve-step program, it is known as the eleventh step prayer and it reads as this:

Lord make me an instrument of your peace.
Where there is hatred, let me sow love;
Where there is injury, pardon;
Where there is doubt, faith;
Where there is despair, hope;
Where there is darkness, light;
Where there is sadness joy.
O' Divine Master, grant that I may not so much seek to be
consoled as to console;
To be understood as to understand;
To be loved as to love;
For it is in giving that we receive;
It is in pardoning that we are pardoned;
It is in dying that we are born again to eternal life, Amen.

I cannot project into the future, for if I do, I am only stealing minutes from the day I have here and now. However, what I can do for today is ask God to "grant me the serenity to accept the things I cannot change; courage to change the things I can; and the wisdom to know the difference."

It is now 2018 and I wish I could tell you I am free from my obsession (the idea or thought that continually preoccupies or intrudes on my mind). Some days are better than others, and I guess that is what they mean when they say, "progress, not perfection." This disease is cunning, baffling, and powerful. Only God's armor will shield me. Thank you, Lord, for your saving grace and your mercy. Every day I am reminded to repeat, "Thy will, not mine, be done," because left to my own defenses, I am lost.

It is imperative for me to remember that at one point in my life, drinking and drugging used to be fun, or so I told myself. I cannot regret the past because it is a part of who I am today.

I thought alcohol made me stronger, prettier, taller, more confident, and brave, but in the end, it stole my freedom. It completely destroyed my life. I became full of denial, lies, and regrets. My many vows to never use again went to the wayside, because the addiction became bigger than me. I no longer had a choice, for my mind and body became so sick that I needed to feed it to stop the ailments of withdrawal. But, God saved my life, again!

We have two courageous cofounders of AA in our history to be grateful for. There is no doubt in my mind that a little over eighty-three years ago God gave a spiritual awakening to one man named Bill W. and he shared his experience with one other drunk, Dr. Bob, and they shared with one more drunkard, Bill D., and that experience brought them to one hundred other men and women who shared their experience with countless others. Bill W. blessed us and left behind him a book called Alcoholics Anonymous, and in this book is our solution for living a sober life. The solution was made simple for us "complicated alcoholics" because we love to make things difficult! In the fifth chapter of the Big Book, known as "How it Works", there is a favorite line of mine, it states: "Remember that we deal with alcohol—cunning, baffling, powerful! Without help, it is too much for us. But there is one who has all power—that one is God. May you find Him now!" Finding God saved my life. Living in His Word brings me peace, and helping others helps keep me sober. This book has aided in saving multitudes of men, women and families. It is meant to be read with a sponsor who has been through it with their sponsor and this is the way to pass on the knowledge that is so freely given.

When I picked my first sponsor, I was more than blessed, and I was willing to sit once a week and read the Big Book and follow through on my steps. They helped me grow out of that frightened five-year-old girl that loved to alter her mind. Following are thoughts on my journey:

Step 1 is my saving grace. It is the only step that I have to do perfectly. This is a three-part step for me, because not only do I have to "admit" to my problem, but I have to "accept" it as well. Then I have to "surrender" daily to the fact that I can no longer safely use any substance.

Step 2 was such a relief. The last words "restore us to sanity" is what caught my attention. My whole life I felt insane, so I was more than willing to believe in something greater than myself.

Step 3 was a real "aha moment" in my life. I was five months into my sobriety when a drink was placed in front of me. Right then and there, I had to make my choice that either God is or He isn't but what was my choice to be. I had a true spiritual awakening on this day, for I finally allowed God into my heart.

Step 4 was a bit scary at first, but after it was completed I felt liberated. It was quite easy to put people's names on a list that wronged me, but I had to look at my part. Where had I been selfish, dishonest, self-seeking, or frightened. I knew I was full of the first three, but I hadn't realized how full of fear I really was.

Step 5 was enlightening. God knew everything about me so when I confessed, He was not surprised, but He was forgiving. This step helped me gain my integrity back. It made me a woman of dignity again. My morals of right and wrong became stable.

Step 6 was a no brainer for me. Now that I knew I had these shortcomings, I was more than ready to release them to God. But mind you, it is not an easy task for me to allow God to remove all my defects. I quite liked some of them because they helped me come to who I am today. However, I believe He removes them in the order they are killing me.

Step 7 is something I do on a daily basis. My character defects love to shine at the worst possible moment, so I must be vigilant of my words and actions. I had to replace all the negative self-talk with God's Fruits of the Spirit: love, joy, peace, patience, kindness, goodness, gentleness, faithfulness, and self-control.

Step 8 is a beginning to cleaning up my side of the street. I already made my list in step four so half of the battle is done for me in this step!

Step 9 is a rewarding step. Of course it's a bit unnerving, but think about it: we truly get to say "I am sorry" and we never have to repeat the behavior again. It is important to remember that amends come in many different forms and when the time comes, God will be with you.

Step 10 is life changing. This step I take throughout my day. At this point, I clearly know right from wrong and my heart will know when it's going astray. I no longer wait for things to build up in me because all the resentment, anger, hatred, fear, self-loathing, all these shortcomings, will take me back into a black hole of craving and compulsion.

Step 11 gives me so much assurance. I am able to communicate with God through prayer and meditation. I can sit quietly and listen for His wisdom; He will answer. But I must be patient, because His timing is not my timing, so I remain still and I breathe.

Step 12 carrying this message to the next addicted fellow is a key ingredient to my sobriety. When I am helping someone, they in return are helping me. This is what keeps my program strong: one fellow-member helping another.

I will remain forever grateful to have a twelve-step program in my life. This is where I started as an infant and grew and grew into the woman God intended me to be. The steps make me stronger and they give me accountability. They also give me light when only darkness follows. I must remember I suffer from a disease that attaches itself to my mind and body. It's insidious and only takes me as a prisoner. Families are broken from the inside out. Satan takes hold and doesn't let go. The evil behind Him grabs me and holds me the minute I stop communing with God, going to meetings, working the steps, and working with others. I must remain acutely aware of my illness while remaining open, honest and willing. I must watch for the days that are filled with pride and ego. I also need to wake every day and hold dear the four absolutes of the Oxford Group of love, honesty, purity, and unselfishness. Although I cannot do any one thing perfectly, I must strive to do my best, and every day, I need to put in God's hands that scared part of me, that five-year-old little girl, that still wants that drink again; not the chaos, but yes, the drink.

My 366-verse journal has been a lifeline to me. It has been a part of my daily tenth step recovery process. I felt the guidance of God as I went along with learning His Word during my therapy writing (turned manuscript). For my sobriety, I love reading through the Bible for encouragement. I also love taking women through the Big Book. In fact, when I am away from either of these for too long, I begin to feel restless. Believe me when I tell you keeping a journal is therapeutic, and I feel is an essential ingredient to our recovery.

Writing isn't always an easy task, however, because it allows us take a look at ourselves in writing and we don't always like what we see! But we do not over think this task, we just do it. Here are some things I considered while journaling in my diary: Think about some of your earliest childhood memories, a special event, or an important day. Maybe your first day at school or your last day. How many siblings you may have. What is your family dynamic? Was it a cohesive unit or was it just individuals living under the same roof? Write about some of your life's accomplishments or what you considered failures. Write about friends, enemies, boyfriends, girlfriends. Write about your youth years, teenage years, adulthood. Was there giving and receiving? Was it balanced or is one stronger than the other? Is there too much pain to bear? Well, write about it! Does your mood depend on what season it is? Is the hustle and bustle of everyday life day after day too much to accept? Are there more questions than there are answers? When we begin writing, we may feel frightened because we are unaware of what we might journal about, but it only brings us insight. It allows us to express ourselves honestly and privately. Try it; remember, we said we would go to any lengths to remain sober!

So I hope you will enjoy the next pages that are filled with how I see recovery. I journal because it allows me to look back with God's wisdom and I can see the changes and differences in my attitude and in my life. God's Word (through our other Big Book) has allowed me to become closer to Him, and I am acutely aware of His spirit that flows gently through me. I know when I am not in sync with God's time, because He gives me subtle reminders. I just have to be waiting and listening. Sobriety happens one day at a time with God. I pray you find Him now, Amen.

Emelia Dooling

Verse 1

"For you have been called to live in freedom, my brothers and sisters. But don't use your freedom to satisfy your sinful nature. Instead, use your freedom to serve one another in love." (Galatians 5:13)

Words for thought:

" We will not regret the past, nor wish to shut the door on it," the Big Book promises, and it is a powerful message to us who suffer from years of self-inflicted pain. We were desperate not to drink, but found ourselves drunk anyway, and then seeing the disapproval and disappointed looks on our loved ones' faces brought us tremendous guilt, shame, and remorse, and we could no longer sit in denial of our disease. So God graciously lead us to find a program of recovery, and we learned through meetings that our past doesn't define who we are today, but it in fact, gives us insight to who we no longer choose to be. See, God uses sinful people all the time and He uses us no matter how broken our life had become. He wants to do good works in our daily life, whatever our past has been. So when we look back in our past, for brief moments, we will always see where God holds us by our right hand as He says to us, "don't be afraid. I am here with you" (Isaiah 41:13).

Let us pray:
Dear Heavenly Father, thank you for your healing hand, Amen.

Verse 2

"For I know the plans I have for you. They are plans for good and not for disaster, to give you a future and a hope." (Jeremiah 29:11)

Words for thought:

B ill Wilson, is the author of the Big Book intended for us to study, learn, and live by its suggestions and must do's. The reading of the book encourages us to *not* pick up that first drink that gets us drunk. It also inspires us to attend meetings regularly, commune with God, clean house, and to practice its principles in all our affairs. In our meetings, we are to step out of our comfort zone and help the next sick and suffering alcoholic. Remembering our duty: "When anyone, anywhere, reaches out for help, I want the hand of AA always to be there. And for that I am responsible."

Let us pray:
Dear Heavenly Father, thank you for allowing me to be of service to you and my fellow members, Amen.

Verse 3

"O Lord, if you heal me, I will be truly healed; if you save me, I will truly be saved. My praises are for you alone!" (Jeremiah 17:14)

Words for thought:

So many of us drank because we didn't know how to let go of the past. We just kept bringing all its garbage back into our daily living and then we would relive all our regrets, and that gave us the excuse to drink ourselves into a self-pitying, drunken stupor. Life will never conform to our expectations of it, but God has created a recovery program for people like us, alcoholics. This program not only teaches us not to drink just for today, but it promises to give us emotional healing, if we do the work. There are steps to follow as a blueprint and a way to clean up our past. And then we get to spread what we learned to the next sick and suffering. Remember, there is so much we do not know and we are trusting God's will over our lives. If we follow our Lord and keep our hope and faith in Him, then His grace will be sufficient for our every need.

Let us pray:
Dear Heavenly Father, thank you Lord for calling me to be one of your chosen, Amen.

Verse 4

"My life is an example to many, because you have been my strength and protection. That is why I can never stop praising you; I declare your glory all day long." (Psalm 71:7-8)

Words for thought:

Through the bafflement of our alcoholism what awaits us is a miracle, and a healing of the mind and body. Our first step is to put down the drink and admit to the fact that we are utterly defeated. Our second step is to unload our mind of all the insanity within and begin with faith to believe there is a God. Our third step is quite clear. It's decision time. Are we going to slide back down the hill of disbelief or skate forward to a brighter future with God? See, if we allow ourselves to gently be led by the Holy Spirit, miraculous things begin to happen. The Lord will lead us out of bondage of self and send us right into the beautiful life He designed for us! Remember, by ourselves we took our own will down the path of destruction. God did not lead us this way, so let us keep our eyes on God, our ears on His promises, and our mouth on His words.

Let us pray:
Dear Heavenly Father, thank you that I no longer have to live in the misery of yesterday, Amen.

Verse 5

*If we claim we have no sin, we are only fooling our-
selves and not living in the truth. But if we confess
our sins to Him, He is faithful and just to forgive us
our sins and to cleanse us from all wickedness, if
we claim we have not sinned, we are calling God a
liar and showing that His Word has no place in our
hearts. (1 John 1:8-10)*

Words for thought:

During our drinking days, we had a prideful attitude. Our
approach to life was to isolate and allow ourselves to become
as drunk as we could before passing out. There was no happy
medium; it was all or nothing. We stifled our emotions because
some of them were unbearable. Once we admitted to our alcoholism, we accepted we cannot drink, just for today. Then we
allowed ourselves to give our will to God and allowed Him to
lead us to sanity. However, we had more work to do to remain
sober. In step four we "made a searching and fearless moral
inventory of ourselves." we discovered we played a role in
every interaction we have with *all* people. The importance of
this step: we look at our behavior. We finally answer the riddle
of where had we been selfish, dishonest, self-seeking, or frightened. We then in step five "admit to God, ourselves, and another
human being the exact nature of our wrongs." Notice it says,
"our wrongs," because this is where we clean up our side of the
street. Our next two steps allow us to become ready and then
humbly come to God to remove our character defects. If we
allow Him, God will remove them in the order they are killing

5

us. Let us not waste time with this process for on the other side, we experience great joy, for our burdens become lighter to carry.

Let us pray:
Dear Heavenly Father, thank you for forgiving what I thought was unforgivable, Amen.

Verse 6

*"Make allowance for each other's faults, and forgive
anyone who offends you. Remember, the Lord forgave
you, so you must forgive others." (Colossians 3:13)*

Words for thought:

OK, so here we go. We've put our alcoholism in God's hands
and we chose to say, "Thy will, not mine, be done." We've
already made the choice of abstinence and decided to go to
any lengths to stay sober. So steps eight and nine should be
easy, right? Not exactly, because making a list of all persons
we had harmed and then resolving to make amends can be quite
the scary task. However, it is said if we skimp on this process, we will surely drink again, someday. So, we ask God for
courage and strength and we push forward. We do not focus
on any wrongs done to us, but only on the need to make right
what we did wrong. *The Twelve Steps and Twelve Traditions*
tells us that we are to "take full consequences of our past acts,
and take responsibility for the well-being of others at the same
time" (p.87).

Let us pray:
*Dear Heavenly Father, thank you for giving me the ability to
mend what had been broken in my relationship with others, Amen.*

Verse 7

"He makes the whole body fit together perfectly. As each part does its own special work, it helps the other parts grow, so that the whole body is healthy and growing and full of love." (Ephesians 4:16)

Words for thought:

There is always four important core pieces to every puzzle. We have the top right and left and then the bottom right and left. In between these cornerstones are the segment pieces that bring us to life. Our alcoholism had these sections of our lives fragmented. In other words, our morals, integrity, and behaviors were far outweighed by our shortcomings of fear, unhappiness, hatred, self-centeredness, and dishonesty. So, how are we to shift our life to fit all the pieces together to work in harmony so we may become whole again? Simple: we work steps ten through twelve on a daily basis so we do not pick up the first drink that gets us drunk. The gift of sobriety is that we become honest, we learn to rely on God for *all* things, we clear our wreckage, we humble ourselves, we make amends, we continue to watch for our ISMS, and finally we pass on the good news to the next alcoholic who still suffers.

Let us pray:
Dear Heavenly Father, thank you for allowing me the privilege to piece my life back together, Amen.

Verse 8

*"This I declare about the Lord; He alone is my refuge,
my place of safety; He is my God, and I trust Him."
(Psalm 91:2)*

Words for thought:

We have to take responsibility for our own drunken behavior. We can say sorry 100 times, and it no longer matters. It is changed behavior that family and friends need to see, hear, and feel from us. Remember, we tormented the lives of others around us. They grieved for us and many thought someday they would be mourning over our bodies. So when the day came in program, we began allowing others to help us until we could help ourselves, and to love us until we could love ourselves. God shined His light upon us and we are not to take this lightly. We are to live in gratitude for His blessings upon us and put our trust in Him, and not rely on ourselves or our own understanding. God is worthy of our undivided attention, so let us stay focused on His plan for us. Pray, meditate, and listen in stillness and He will lead.

Let us pray:
Dear Heavenly Father, thank you for hearing my cry for mercy, Amen.

Verse 9

"You will keep in perfect peace all who trust in you,
all whose thoughts are fixed on you." (Isaiah 26:3)

Words for thought:

How brilliant is God's promise! When drinking, we had no hope and the future was blurred, but step one says admit you're powerless over alcohol and that your life had become unmanageable. Steps two and three brought us before our loving God to make a decision: God either is or He isn't, what was our choice to be (p.53 BB). Take a moment and think about it: we have faith in all the material world, so why not change our spiritual world?

Let us pray:
Dear Heavenly Father, thank you for being there for me when I could not be there for myself. You saved me, Lord, and I thank you, Amen.

Verse 10

"Trouble chases sinners, while blessings reward the righteous." (Proverbs 13:10)

Words for thought:

For some of us, during our drinking career we had a bad attitude. We've had this viewpoint from as far back as we could remember and we didn't know we had a choice to change. Hell, we alcoholics don't like change to begin with and now ten, twenty, thirty years later you want us to adjust our perspective and believe that nothing in God's world is by mistake? The answer to that question is *yes*! You see, some of us were knocked down more times than we care to count. For some, we had a great upbringing and for others, most of life's problems we created by our own drinking drama. But no matter how the past was, we have the ability to adjust our thinking by God's Word. This approach to life isn't always easy, but it is necessary. It is called accepting the things we cannot change!

Let us pray:
Dear Heavenly Father, thank you that I no longer have to think as the child I once was, Amen.

Verse 11

"For all people are like grass, and all their glory is like the flowers of the field; the grass withers and the flowers fall, but the word of the Lord endures forever."
(1 Peter 1:24)

Words for thought:

Everything in this world is temporary except God's Word. That is awesome news! God's Word is our security. We can celebrate with joy, hope, and confidence. We are free to worship His holy name and show gratitude for all He has saved us from. We were once in the snares of alcoholism, but as soon as God heard our plea, He saved us. He loosened the chains of all evil surrounding us while we were drowning in our addiction. He alone helped heal our thoughts so we could move past our obsession.

Let us pray:
Dear Heavenly Father, thank you that your Word endures forever because you promise eternal life, Amen.

Verse 12

*"Help me abandon my shameful ways; for your reg-
ulations are good. I long to obey your commandments! Renew my life with Your goodness." (Psalm
119:39-40)*

Words for thought:

In our alcoholic behavior, we showed extreme selfishness. We
couldn't possibly love God or others, because we could not
love ourselves. We ignored the interest and needs of family to
gain self-satisfaction in the bottle. At our best, we were egotistical, self-centered, greedy, and self-indulgent. But thanks to
our time in fellowship and with God, the moment came in our
sobriety when we could leave all those things behind and look
to the future with new-found love, gratitude, and humility. God
tells us in Scripture not to be selfish and He also tells us not to
try to impress others. He wants us to be humble, thinking of
others as better than ourselves. He says not to look at our own
interest, but to take an interest in others too (Philippians 2:3-
4). So let's spend time in God's Word and watch the amazing
things soon to unfold!

Let us pray:
*Dear Heavenly Father, thank you for giving me the discipline
in seeking your Word, Amen.*

Verse 13

*"Turn away from evil and do good. Search for peace,
and work to maintain it." (1 Peter 3:11)*

Words for thought:

" Acceptance is the key to all my problems today," is what it tells us in the Big Book! And we will find no peace until we accept every person, place, or thing being exactly as it is today. This is a huge deal for us alcoholics, because it's renewing our mind and heart from everything we thought we knew. So just saying no to the alcohol was not enough, because God wanted to get to know us personally. See, God already knows our beginning to our end, but we play a role here, and that is to remain strong in our spirituality, prayer time, and faith. If we are obedient to Him, He will supply us with the wisdom to know the difference and He will offer us a sober life.

Let us pray:
Dear Heavenly Father, thank you for your wisdom that I can do today what I will not regret later, Amen.

Verse 14

"But let all who take refuge in you rejoice; let them sing joyful praises forever. Spread your protection over them, that all who love your name may be filled with joy. For You bless the godly, O Lord; you surround them with your shield of love." (Psalm 5:11-12)

Words for thought:

When we finally put the drink down we were able to stop living in conflict within ourselves. God provides us with the means we need to stay sober. However, we must pray and ask Him for patience, knowledge, and guidance to find our way back to Him and living. We must humble ourselves daily in step seven where it says, "Humbly asked Him to remove our shortcomings." Our souls will be renewed and we must let others see it in our actions, thoughts, and words so others will want what we have.

Let us pray:
Dear Heavenly Father, thank you for the life you have provided me. You have offered me a life of sobriety and I am grateful, Amen.

Verse 15

"So you must live as God's obedient children. Don't slip back into your old ways of living to satisfy your own desires. You didn't know any better." (1 Peter 1:14)

Words for thought:

O ur lives were shattered by our alcoholism. We created such woe and desolation to our lives and to the lives of our loved ones. This created in us guilt, shame, and remorse which overwhelmed us and kept us drinking day after day. We believed we deserved to live a life of misery, isolation, and regrets. Satan had us on a path of destruction. We believed His lies and so we continued this addictive cycle of emotional drinking. But we can rest assure that we will remain captive to our alcoholism until we get rigorously honest with ourselves and admit we are alcoholic. From there we surrender to God so we can be clothed in His armor, and once that is underway, then God can heal our once hopeless condition, and Satan has no choice but to flee!

Let us pray:
Dear Heavenly Father, thank you for plucking me out of the snare of all evil, Amen.

Verse 16

"The Lord is good to those who depend on Him, to those who search Him. So it is good to wait quietly for salvation from the Lord." (Lamentations 3:25-26)

Words for thought:

Isn't it so magnificent that all we have to do is be quiet and in the stillness, we hear God's Word? We hear Him because we put the drink down and slowly began our recovery. We mustered the courage to work our twelve-step program, which taught us how to live spiritually fit. But now we must work and show others what God has done in our heart and we begin by giving away that which we received: hope in sobriety! What is important here is that we know that everything is in God's time. So, when we haven't received an answer to what we want, then we are to wait patiently until it is clear what our next action should be. See, rushing forward without God is not only foolish, but can be ruinous to our sobriety. So what do we do? We wait on the Lord bravely and courageously and we trust that His timing will reveal the answers, whether it be slowly or suddenly; we wait patiently for Him!

Let us pray:
Dear Heavenly Father, thank you that I no longer have to stand in this world alone, Amen.

Verse 17

"The Lord is close to all who call on Him, yes, to all who call on Him in truth. He grants the desires of those who fear Him; He hears their cries for help and He rescues them. The Lord protects all those who love Him, but He destroys the wicked." (Psalm 145:18-20)

Words for thought:

Soon into recovery we become aware that our compulsion to drink has been lifted, and that we are offered a new sense of freedom, even if it is just for today. There are going to be days when we feel hopeless, discouraged, and want to give into our disease, but this feeling will soon pass as we begin to count out all our blessings. God will strengthen us through many trials and tribulations in our lifetime. So, let us boldly put all our faith, all our hope, and all our trust in the hands of God and simply believe that on our road to recovery, God will work all things according to His will and purpose for our lives.

Let us pray:
Dear Heavenly Father, thank you for helping me see that my memories are not the enemy, but through them I have wisdom to know the difference, Amen.

Verse 18

*"This is my command-be strong and courageous! Do
not be afraid or discouraged. For the Lord your God
is with you wherever you go." (Joshua 1:9)*

Words for thought:

Did you know that we do not have to clean up our act before
we go to God? He tells us to come as we are! Not only will
He accept us, but He will save us. The great news is that we
only have to believe in our heart and in His Word that He is our
one true Father. So no matter what you are facing today, God is
right there and He promises us in Psalm 91:3 to rescue us from
every trap and that He will protect us from deadly disease—our
disease of alcoholism.

Let us pray:
*Dear Heavenly Father, thank you that you have filled my life
with such wonderful people, Amen.*

Verse 19

"He saved us, not because of the righteous things we had done, but because of His mercy. He washed away our sins, giving us new birth and a new life through the Holy Spirit." (Titus 3:5)

Words for thought:

We need to spend time in prayer. The only thing we should dwell on in life is God's Word. We must repent and surrender to Him, for He wants to give us a daily reprieve from our alcoholism. He has a glorious life for us to live, if we so choose, and when any kind of trouble comes our way, we can consider it an opportunity for great joy because our faith is tested, and our endurance has a chance to grow (James 1:2-3).

Let us pray:
Dear Heavenly Father, thank you for this day. Show me how to live life on your terms, Lord, Amen.

Verse 20

"So do not fear, for I am with you; do not be dismayed, for I am your God. I will strengthen you and help you; I will uphold you with my righteous right hand." (Isaiah 41:10)

Words for thought:

We are the ones who determine how close we want to be to God. He patiently waits for a relationship with us. Our alcoholism kept us in the snares of Satan for far too long. He tempted and taunted us every day with our addiction and He won day in and day out. But remember, God blesses those of us who patiently endure testing and temptation, and afterward, we will receive the crown of life that He has promised to those who love Him (James 1:12). He created us to live in fellowship with one another, to love one another. The time we spend with Him can be endless.

Let us pray:
Dear Heavenly Father, I thank you for this day. Please bring me closer to you with each passing hour, Amen.

Verse 21

"I the Lord search the heart and examine the mind, to reward each person according to their conduct, according to what their deeds deserve." (Jeremiah 17:10)

Words for thought:

Our minds were tortured by our disease. We wanted to quit, truly, but we just could not escape its trap. The shakes, the vomiting, the falling down, the slurred speech, the angry outbursts were all a part of our everyday existence, but there is a solution. We may not feel comfortable about the truth of it because it involves abstinence and God, but these two things only brings us to the truth. We must face life's challenges, admit to them, accept them, and allow them to change us, one day at a time. We are to trust the Lord with all of our heart and we must not depend on our own understanding. For if we seek His will in all we do, He will show us which path to take (Proverbs 3:5-6).

Let us pray:
Dear Heavenly Father, Thank you for your guidance that I will receive today. Please help me with the truths of life, Amen.

Verse 22

"I love you, Lord; you are my strength. The Lord is my rock, my fortress, and my Savior; my God is my rock, in whom I find protection. He is my shield, the power that saves me, and my place of safety." (Psalm 18:1-2)

Words for thought:

For far too long we needed to rest in the Lord. Our souls were crying, and we were drowning. The alcohol had us in its chains. We were suffering from our own transgressions. We know it is not the of making God, but that of our own willpower. We need to be willing to put all our truth, all our sins, all our faith, and all our hope in Him. We can believe that God never grows weary and that He will continue showering us with His goodness, His strength, and His wisdom. He will teach us, guide us, love us, and shelter us in His Word all the day long because our hearts have bled for too long.

Let us pray:
Dear Heavenly Father, thank you for hearing my cry for help, Amen.

Verse 23

"May the God of hope fill you with all joy and peace
as you trust Him, so that you may overflow with hope
by the power of the Holy Spirit." (Romans 15:13)

Words for thought:

G od saved our lives. He has forgiven our sins. He wants to protect us so let us obey His Word and do good in our lives. We must allow God to influence our faith so we may do good to one another. We must not be afraid to show others how gracious God has been to us. We are to "reach out our hand anytime, anywhere when someone reaches out for help" because there are millions more who suffer from this insidious disease of alcoholism and they do not know that God is waiting for them. We are to show our faith to draw others near to Him. Let us never forget His goodness and faithfulness.

Let us pray:
Dear Heavenly Father, I lift up those who have turned against you. I pray that they may change their ways and receive the gift of sobriety, Amen.

Verse 24

"Such things were written in the scriptures long ago to teach us. And the Scriptures give us hope and encouragement as we wait patiently for God's promises to be fulfilled." (Romans 15:4)

Words for thought:

Recovery is not just about saying no to the bottle. It is an opportunity for us to desire a brand-new way of life. It is us wanting a fresh start full of God and His wisdom. Scripture encourages us to hold tightly without wavering and to never give up or let go, and to always have hope, because God can be trusted to keep His promises (Hebrews 10:23). We are to be careful, because are living in a world full of all kinds of evil, temptations, and filth, but if we choose we can humbly accept the Word of God that He has planted in our hearts, because it has the power to save our souls (James 1:21).

Let us pray:
Dear Heavenly Father, thank you for my brand-new beginning, Amen.

Verse 25

"For I am the Lord your God who takes hold of your right hand and says to you, do not fear; I will help you." (Isaiah 41:13)

Words for thought:

K now this, God made every delicate, inner parts of our body because He knit us in our mother's womb (Psalm 139:13), so He already knows that we are coming to Him weak and wounded. This knowledge allows us to freely ask Him to lift our alcoholic burden. We do not have to suffer or be afraid any longer because He forgives us our trespasses. When God lifted our obsession to drink He gave us the gift of life, but remember: what we have received, we must give away.

Let us pray:
Dear Heavenly Father, thank you for giving me your Word so I may spread the good news to my fellow members, Amen.

Verse 26

*"You've made me; you created me. Now give me the
sense to follow your commands." (Psalm 119:73)*

Words for thought:

In life we need to remember to build our foundation on God and
for God, because He began a great work in us when He called
for us to be saved—saved from an alcoholic death. Entering
into our program we soon discovered that unless we are "spiritually fit" we will someday drink again, and that is why How it
Works from the Big Book Alcoholics Anonymous states, "We
thought we could find an easier, softer way. But we could not.
With all the earnestness at our command, we beg of you to be
fearless and thorough from the very start." We cannot afford
the luxury of half measures because alcohol is "cunning, baffling, and powerful." We get it, we live in a broken world and
we know that we will suffer, but if we pray to God for courage,
strength, and endurance, He will provide. He says because of
our faith, Christ has brought us into a place of undeserved privilege where we now stand, and we confidently and joyfully look
forward to sharing God's glory. He continues by saying that
we can also rejoice, too, when we run into problems and trials,
for we know they help us develop endurance. And endurance
develops strength of character, and character strengthens our
confident hope of salvation. And this hope will not lead to disappointment. For we know how dearly God loves us, because
He has given us the Holy Spirit to fill our hearts with His love
(Romans 5:2-5).

Let us pray:
Dear Heavenly Father, thank you for allowing me to bring my problems to you because nothing is too small or too big for you, Amen.

Verse 27

*"Make a tree good, and then its fruit will be good
or make a tree rotten, and then its fruit will be
rotten. A person can recognize a tree by its fruits."
(Matthew 12:33)*

Words for thought:

Today is a beautiful day! We no longer have to be consumed with the worrying thoughts of when we're going to drink or how much we're going to drink. We do not have to hide our bottles from family members. We don't have to fear that we are going to get behind the wheel of a car and kill ourselves or others. All we are responsible for today is to lift our eyes to God and just thank Him for His saving grace. We can thank Him because our hearts are full of love, joy, faith, trust, courage, hope, perseverance, strength, purpose, and forgiveness. So whatever we do today, whether in word or action, it should be to represent God.

Let us pray:
*Dear Heavenly Father, thank you for your special gift of the
Holy Spirit; we are undeserving but you love us that much, Amen.*

Verse 28

"This is my command-be strong and courageous! Do not be afraid or discouraged. For the Lord your God is with you wherever you go." (Joshua 1:9)

Words for thought:

We are powerless over our addictions and compulsive behaviors. Our life was unmanageable. We needed a power greater than ourselves to restore us to sanity and AA brought us this solution. We found the one who allows us to lift our head high again. We found God who keeps us safe, who shields us from danger, who grants us wisdom and gives us understanding. We are to give all glory to Him who saved us from the power of all darkness.

Let us pray:
Dear Heavenly Father, thank you for saving me by your grace, Amen.

Verse 29

"The soul of the lazy person has strong desires but gets nothing, but the soul of the one who does his best gets more than he needs." (Proverbs 13:4)

Words for thought:

At a time in our life, we found ourselves dead because of our sins. We drank and followed our sinful ways all the way into darkness. We obeyed Satan and not God. We continually lived in the past, all its mistakes and regrets blocked our path and would not allow us to move forward to our future. We were sick physically, mentally, and spiritually. But by God's loving favor, we have been saved from the punishment of sin through our faith. The day we committed ourselves to our sobriety, God gave us His blessing. He granted us the ability to work hard at His Word so we can enjoy His fruits. Remember God's love goes beyond anything we can possibly understand here on this earth. So let us keep wisdom in all our decision making while keeping God at the center of our universe.

Let us pray:
Dear Heavenly Father, I want to thank you for today and for helping me declare that I have victory in you, Amen.

Verse 30

"Dear brothers and sisters, when troubles of any kind come your way, consider it an opportunity for great joy. For you know that when your faith is tested, your endurance has a chance to grow." (James 1:2-3)

Words for thought:

Our mind, will, and emotions were all jammed up and we couldn't think anymore. Our mind was so corroded with stinking thinking and we were so full of self, all God could do was wait patiently for us to surrender. Thankfully there came that day in our sickness when we were just sick and tired that we crumbled and pleaded to Him, "God, please help me!" He heard our plea and granted us the wisdom to know the difference.

Let us pray:
Dear Heavenly Father, thank you for saving me. You not only spared me, but you sent your only Son to die for me and I am eternally grateful, Amen.

Verse 31

*"For the spirit of God gave us does not make us timid,
but gives us power, love, and self-discipline." (2
Timothy 1:7)*

Words for thought:

Sometimes it is confusing knowing that God has created us all on purpose, for a purpose. I know today that God did not want me to choose the path of drunkenness and drugs. Thank the heavens that Bill Wilson, Dr. Bob, and Bill D, number three, saw this addiction as a weakness in our character. They experienced the same kind of insanity that brought us all to our knees in the hands of God. God gives us hope, strength, guidance, courage, love, purpose, and mercy. Having a relationship with God is not complicated. We simply call upon Him in prayer and we listen through quiet time to hear what He placed on our hearts.

Let us pray:
Dear Heavenly Father, thank you for saving my soul. Eighty-two years ago you opened the door of AA for many to walk through, Amen.

Verse 32

"But you, O Lord, are a shield for me, my glory, and the one who lifts up my head." (Psalm 3:3)

Words for thought:

God graces us with strength. Living the life He has called us to live sober can be difficult, but the battle truly is not the end, but only the beginning. When we stand firm in our prayers, spirituality, and faith, God will nourish us, one day at a time. But be warned: if we should rest on our own laurels, we will be headed for trouble!

Let us pray:
Dear Heavenly Father, thank you for your shield around me that protects me and brings me strength, Amen.

Verse 33

"Submit yourselves, then, to God. Resist the devil, and he will flee from you. Come near to God and He will come near to you. Wash your hands, you sinners, and purify your hearts, you double minded." (James 4:7-8)

Words for thought:

Think about it: sometimes just waking up is harrowing. Our minds wander into that deep thought of ungratefulness, and then we remember our disease. The sickness that wants us back into that deep bottom of despair. One day at a time, we must work tirelessly with God, in His Word, to seek love, kindness, and mercy because God opposes the proud but He will give grace to the humble.

Let us pray:
Dear Heavenly Father, thank you for saving me from my agonizing days and giving me rest, Amen.

Verse 34

Humble yourselves, therefore, under God's mighty hand, that He may lift you up in due time. Cast all your anxiety on Him because He cares about you." (1 Peter 5:6-7)

Words for thought:

Do circumstances fill our minds with doubt? Yes, because Satan is nipping at our heals every step of the way. He wants us to surrender to our disease. God, however, says, "Have faith in me, put all your trust in me." The Lord waits patiently for us to surrender our mind, will, and emotions to Him. No matter our circumstances, we pray, we meditate, and we remain quiet, patiently staying focused on the Lord.

Let us pray:
Dear Heavenly Father, thank you for being a part of who I am today because you have sent the Holy Spirit to live in me, Amen.

Verse 35

"Finally, brothers and sisters, whatever is true, whatever is noble, whatever is right, whatever is pure, whatever is lovely, whatever is admirable-if anything is excellent or praiseworthy-think about such things." (Philippians 4:8)

Words for thought:

As we journey into our day with thanksgiving, we must stop and give gratitude. No matter our life conditions, we must remember that we have been given the gift of sobriety by God's grace. We are given the twelve steps to become honest, humbled, giving, tolerant, loving, and forgiving people to those around us. With every deep breath we are to give thanks to our Lord for saving us from dying a death that Satan had planned for us.

Let us pray:
Dear Heavenly Father, thank you for surrounding me with people who get it, Amen.

Verse 36

"Trust the Lord with all your heart; do not depend on your own understanding. Seek His will in all you do, and he will show you which path to take." (Proverbs 3:5-6)

Words for thought:

In our drinking hours, we opened the door for Satan to enter our life, and He encouraged us to worry about the things we could change. But God tells us to be "sober, be vigilant; because your adversary the devil walks about like a roaring lion, seeking whom He may devour" (1 Peter 5:8). God did not call us to a lifetime of drunkenness, sadness, and frustration. He calls us to be happy, joyous, and free. Our Lord has everything under His control; remember it is thy will be done, not mine!

Let us pray:
Dear Heavenly Father, thank you that I can cast all my cares on you. You are the light of this world, Amen.

Verse 37

"The Lord Himself goes before you and will be with you; He will never leave you nor forsake you. Do not be afraid; do not be discouraged." (Deuteronomy 31:8)

Words for thought:

God helps keep us sober. Every day, we petition, "please keep me away from a drink or drug today." We must believe there is nothing more important than knowing that God is our top priority in life. Daily we are to wait on our Lord and then we meditate, reflect, and ponder His Word. We live the life offered to us in the twelve steps of Alcoholics Anonymous, and if there is an area in our life that God needs to correct, then we pray for His guidance, and He will give us the courage to change the things we can.

Let us pray:
Dear Heavenly Father, thank you for always being my number one, Amen.

Verse 38

"The faithful love of the Lord never ends! His mercies never cease. Great is His faithfulness; His mercies begin afresh each morning. I say to myself, the Lord is my inheritance; therefore, I will hope in Him." (Lamentations 3:22-24)

Words for thought:

L ord, we ask you to help us stay away from a drink or drug today. Please help us to follow your commands that will keep us free from bondage of self. Please give us the wisdom so we may help others be empowered with your Word. We want to follow the narrow path that you offer us that leads to your perfect love. When we come to that fork in the road where we have to choose between A and B, help us stay grounded in your presence and grant us the courage to continually follow the path that leads to our recovery, not the road that will lead to our addiction of demise.

Let us pray:
Dear Heavenly Father, thank you for guiding me when it came time for me to make you my inheritance, Amen.

Verse 39

And may you have the power to understand, as all God's people should, how wide, how long, how high, and how deep his love is. May you experience the love of Christ, though it is too great to understand fully. Then you will be made complete with all the fullness of life and power that comes from God. (Ephesians 3:18-19)

Words for thought:

We can rest knowing that with God there is always a way. Sometimes our circumstances may not be easy or convenient, but we have been told as long as we keep our faith, our gratitude, and our thankfulness in Him, He will see us through, even on our darkest days. We must understand it may not be as quickly as we desire, but nonetheless, we can believe that God is always on time! Remember, through Him all things are possible!

Let us pray:
Dear Heavenly Father, may I always believe, till the end of time, your love for me, Amen.

Verse 40

*"God has given each of you a gift from His variety of
spiritual gifts. Use them well to serve one another."
(1 Peter 4:10)*

Words of thought:

Step seven says to "humbly ask Him to remove our shortcomings." If we allow God, He will take our failures and
weaknesses, our faults and our sins. He will take our disease
and our failed past and replace these things with His love. We
must know this: God is a merciful God who showers us with
forgiveness and He gives us the fruits of the spirit (Galatians
5:22-23) to live by. So what does He expect from us in return?
God wants us to do what is right, He wants us to love mercy,
and He wants us to walk humbly with Him.

Let us pray:
*Dear Heavenly Father, thank you for your fruits. They fill my
life with hope, Amen.*

Verse 41

"Praise be to the Lord our Savior, who daily bears our burdens." (Psalm 68:19)

Words for thought:

In our fellowship, we learn to release the control factor. We release trying to be manipulative. We finally let go and let God! We allow our spiritual journey with the Holy Spirit give us guidance and serenity. We persevere under trials and tribulations to reach our greatest purpose by working the twelve steps and helping our fellow member. We do all these things to remain sober just one more day.

Let us pray:
Dear Heavenly Father, thank you for the hands you lift me up with, Amen.

Verse 42

"Put on all God's armor so that you will be able to stand firm against all strategies of the devil." (Ephesians 6:11)

Words for thought:

We have all worn a mask to cover up our illness. We felt that we were not good enough, worthy enough, or loved enough, so we drank. But in the fellowship, little by little, we found we could remove the mask because we were just sick people living in the world of alcoholism. We discovered we were honest people just trying to get better. We were willing enough to go to any length to stay sober and fight the evil within. We found hope, hope in God, that with each day we could love ourselves for the first time in our lives. We became people that could be trusted by family and friends again, as long as we do not pick up that first drink.

Let us pray:
Dear Heavenly Father, thank you for standing strong for me and waiting patiently until I was ready to come to you, Amen.

Verse 43

"Now faith is the substance of things hoped for, the evidence of things not seen." (Hebrews 11:1)

Words for thought:

Dipping our toes in the water of faith is just a beginning. At some place and time we all come to a place in the river where we must cross the waters. God tells us not to be afraid because He is with us. He says do not be discouraged, for He is our God. He promises to strengthen and help us and He tells us He will hold us up with His victorious right hand (Isaiah 41:10). God will carry us through the calm and the calamity. Through all this we can believe by faith and not by sight.

Let us pray:
Dear Heavenly Father, I close my eyes and I speak to you and you bring me such comfort, thank you, Amen.

Verse 44

"If you love me, keep my command." (John 14:15)

Words for thought:

When and how we obey God is when the Lord instructs you to do so. This timely obedience will not only affect you, but it will impact others in our circle of life. When we look back in hindsight, we can see exactly when God saved us. We all have had a spiritual experience that Bill W. speaks of. Some awakenings are subtle, while others are profound. Either way, it has influenced our lives and attitudes greatly! The Lord tells us through Matthew 7:7 to "keep on asking and you will receive what you ask for. Keep on seeking and you will find. Keep on knocking, and the door will be opened to you." We never give up and neither will God!

Let us pray:
Dear Heavenly Father, thank you for your guidance for today and all to come, Amen.

Verse 45

"If any of you lacks wisdom, you should ask God, who gives generously to all without finding fault, and it will be given to you." (James 1:5)

Words for thought:

We may not always feel comfortable about the truth God brings us, but we must do our part. We must accept it, and allow Him to change us. God is the only one who showers blessings on us, and He will turn any circumstance around for our good. He has saved us all from an alcoholic death, and called us to a higher purpose. So we must have complete trust and confidence in Him at all times while spreading His wonderful word! Hallelujah!

Let us pray:
Dear Heavenly Father, thank you for always turning my mess into a message, Amen.

Verse 46

"Joyful are people of integrity, who follow the instructions of the Lord. Joyful are those who obey His laws and search for Him with all their hearts. They do not compromise with evil, and they walk only in His paths." (Psalm 119:1-3)

Words for thought:

Only our God knows the purpose for our life. When we allow Him, He will keep us and guide us on the narrow path where we will enter His kingdom. He tells us the highway to hell is broad, and its gate is wide for the many who choose that way (Matthew 7:13) and for us, who have traveled that broad alcoholic highway once, know that we must choose to stay true to God's journey. We must go in faith knowing that we never have to come to that drunk fork in the road again, as long as we make the choice to stay away from a drink one day at a time.

Let us pray:
Dear Heavenly Father, thank you for clearing a sober path for me to journey. Amen.

Verse 47

"But if we confess our sins to Him, He is faithful and just to forgive us our sins and to cleanse us from all wickedness." (1 John 1:9)

Words for thought:

So they tell us in the program that acceptance is the key to all our problems. That all through these years we have built up fear and resentments. The fellowship tells us there is only one power who can relieve us of all our anxieties and drunkenness if we are only willing to follow twelve steps. Wow, all we have to do is surrender to a power greater than ourselves and we will find great treasures on the other side. No more misery, contempt, and self-loathing. No more dishonesty, manipulation, torment, and rebellion. No more complaining, grumbling, or self-pity. If we are willing to put down the drink and follow God's commands and let go of what used to be, then we can live a good, clean, honest, sober life. And best of all, we only have to do this one day at a time!

Let us pray:
Dear Heavenly Father, thank you for allowing me to start this day open-minded, willingly, and honestly, Amen.

Verse 48

"But the Holy Spirit produces this kind of fruit in our lives: love, joy, peace, patience, kindness, goodness, gentleness, and self-control. There is no law against these things." (Galatians 5:22-23)

Words for thought:

How awesome it is to have step seven in our lives where we ask God to humbly remove our shortcomings! We already have His promises waiting for us in Galatians of what we receive in return, so why live in the bottle with all its guilt, shame, and remorse. In our sobriety we no longer lay with Satan because God promises "He will fight for us, and all we have to be is silent" (Exodus 14:14).

Let us pray:
Dear Heavenly Father, thank you for your Scripture. Please help me to move graciously forward in your Word, Amen.

Verse 49

*"Show me the right path, O Lord; point out the road
for me to follow." (Psalm 25:4)*

Words for thought:

We have two ways to confront a situation: the world's way or
God's way! God is always present, reliable, and true and
we need His Word and wisdom. Unfortunately, we chose the
world's way by staying in the bondage of self while indulging
in drinking until we either lost everything or came pretty damn
close to losing it all. We trusted our feelings instead of the way
God said, which was to "walk by the spirit, and you will not
gratify the desires of the flesh" (Galatians 5:16).

Let us pray:
*Dear Heavenly Father, thank you for giving me your words to
live by, Amen.*

Verse 50

"Yet what we suffer now is nothing compared to the glory He will reveal to us later." (Romans 8:18)

Words for thought:

Once we become sober, there are still times in our day that we feel ourselves plunging deep into disbelief and turmoil. Satan torments us daily with impatience, anger, and negativity. But our program gives us steps to remember that we already made the decision to turn our will and our lives over to the care of God as we understood Him, and we know that God's Word gives us all the solutions. We must not believe the enemy's lies, lest we drink again.

Let us pray:
Dear Heavenly Father, thank you for the reward that you have waiting for me, Amen.

Verse 51

"Those who live according to the flesh have their minds set on what the flesh desires; but those who live in accordance with the Spirit have their minds set on what the Spirit desires. The mind governed by the Spirit is life and peace." (Romans 8:5-6)

Words for thought:

God has given us our own will to live by! We can live life by the world's standards or by God's Word. Think about it: we lived with our lower power, Satan, the whole time we drank. Day after day, we ultimately had the power of choice, but our bodies became just as sick as our minds so we had to feed it; or did we? No, because God gave us a solution to stay clean and sober. He gave us the gift of sobriety and the opportunity to have a clean slate every twenty-four hours! So let us choose today to live by the spirit and not the flesh.

Let us pray:
Dear Heavenly Father, thank you for my choice to choose good or evil, right or wrong, Amen.

Verse 52

"Death and life are in the power of the tongue;
those who love to talk will reap the consequences."
(Proverbs 18:21)

Words for thought:

During our alcoholism sprees, whatever we thought would come distastefully out of our mouths. We would lash out at anyone who would try to help us with our disease. We would soon learn in our program that we must not allow our emotions to control our actions. We learn to carefully control our words when we feel angry, rejected, or simply when our feelings get hurt. If we pray, God will give us enough wisdom to say things quietly and softly.

Let us pray:
Dear Heavenly Father, thank you for helping me be nice today, Amen.

Verse 53

"So I say, let the Holy Spirit guide your lives. Then you won't be doing what your sinful nature craves." (Galatians 5:16)

Words for thought:

One of the things we learn from the rooms and ultimately from God is self-control. It literally comes to play in every aspect of our lives. We need to discipline ourselves so our emotions do not overrule us. Remember: emotions are fickle and can sometimes be out of balance. Self-control is a Fruit of the Spirit we develop over time, so when we choose to follow the lead of the Holy Spirit, we will experience victory in our own self-control.

Let us pray:
Dear Heavenly Father, thank you for this fruit. Just knowing it is a true part of who I am relieves my worries, Amen.

Verse 54

"The Lord is compassionate and merciful, slow to get angry and filled with unfailing love. He will not constantly accuse us, nor remain angry forever. He does not punish us for all our sins; He does not deal harshly with us, as we deserve." (Psalm 103:8-10)

Words for thought:

We need to wake with a thankful heart because God is teaching us to think of others and not just ourselves. He instructs us daily of how to be kind and tenderhearted. He shows us how to forgive, for we have been forgiven. We have been so unkind to ourselves through years and years of drinking. Our minds were polluted with thoughts of not wanting to be who we were because, after all, we were plain old drunks. But God's light shone upon us and we were able to reach a higher priority for our lives. We realized we no longer have to be angry for what we did or what we said or who we hurt because once we abstained from our addiction God transformed our heart and made all things new.

Let us pray:
Dear Heavenly Father, thank you for being so merciful and gracious for all my sins, Amen.

Verse 55

"For we live by faith, not by sight."
(2 Corinthians 5:7)

Words for thought:

We need not worry or be anxious for anything. For we can pray about everything, big or small. Remember, God is ultimate, boundless, and unconditional. While some things are too big for us, nothing is too big for Him. He called for us to surrender our alcoholism to Him, because He is our Lord. We are His clay and He is the potter. We all are formed by His hand (Isaiah 64:8).

Let us pray:
Dear Heavenly Father, thank you that you hear me when I call your Holy name, for once I was near death and now I am saved, Amen.

Verse 56

"Those who are dominated by the sinful nature think about sinful things, but those who are controlled by the Holy Spirit think about things that please the Spirit. So letting your sinful nature control your mind leads to death. But letting the Spirit control your mind leads to life and peace." (Romans 8:5-7)

Words for thought:

Praise and worship the God of heaven, thanking Him for His Son, His grace, and His mercy. It is by a spiritual change that our lives have been spared and because of this, all the glory belongs to the Father. God knows our pain, our struggles, our doubts, and our shame, but He gives us peace and purpose anyway for our lives. All these things may seem impossible, but not for our Most High.

Let us pray:
Dear Heavenly Father, thank you that you allowed your only begotten Son to die on the cross for me, Amen.

Verse 57

"We are pressed on every side by troubles, but we are not crushed. We are perplexed, but not driven to despair. We are hunted down, but never abandoned by God. We get knocked down but we are not destroyed." (2 Corinthians 4:8-9)

Words for the day:

A s we go through our day, we can be sure that life is uncertain and we are not in control. If we chase temporary happiness in the bottle, our happiness will quickly fade. True serenity comes as a gift from God. Think about it, our true contentment is in sobriety, and it all comes from God.

Let us pray:
Dear Heavenly Father, thank you that for today I do not need a substance to complete me, Amen.

Verse 58

"For the Lord grants wisdom! From His mouth come knowledge and understanding." (Proverbs 2:6)

Words for thought:

D ecisions will be called for today and we will be faced with numerous choices. However, we must be careful of our emotions because they can sometimes lead us astray and wreak havoc in or lives. We had been so accustomed to our judgment being impaired by alcohol that it was hard to break free from our emotions. So where do we find the balance and guidance to our daily decisions? Well, we listen closely for counsel that comes from God and His Word, because He tells us, "fix your thoughts on what is true, and honorable, and right, and pure, and lovely, and admirable. Think about things that are excellent and worthy of praise" (Philippians 4:8). Let us be patient in our decisiveness and then give all the glory to God.

Let us pray:
Dear Heavenly Father, thank you for helping me make my options clear in your Word, Amen.

Verse 59

*"And thou shall love the Lord your God with all your
heart, and with all thy soul, and with all thy might."
(Luke 10:27)*

Words for thought:

In our suffering we closed off any communication we had with
God. Oh, we would pray "foxhole" prayers while intoxicated,
then soon returned to our sinful ways. When we faced trials and
tribulations, we always turned to the bottle instead of God, and
He just watched and waited for us to come back to Him. We
were living in our own will with much suffering until the day
He saved us. On that day, He flooded us with mercy, hope, love,
grace, and purpose while we sang:

"Our Father who art in heaven hallowed be your name. Thy
kingdom come, thy will be done in earth as it is in heaven. Give
us this day, our daily bread, and forgive us our trespasses as we
forgive those who trespass against us, lead us not into temptation but deliver us from evil, for thine is the kingdom and the
power and the glory forever and ever, Amen."

Let us pray:
*Dear Heavenly Father, thank you for giving me exactly what I
need when I need it, Amen.*

Verse 60

"Give generously to Him and do so without a grudging heart; then because of this the Lord your God will bless you in all your work and in everything you put your hand to." (Deuteronomy 15:10)

Words for thought:

We should always and abundantly be giving thanks to God for all of His goodness in our lives. We must be watchful, because there is countless temptations threatening our faith in Him. He knows how difficult it is, at times, for us to remain loyal to our sobriety, but that is why it is about the progress not the perfection. The words of Proverbs 4:20-27 give us comfort in knowing we can move forward to a life of hope, purpose, growth, healing, and thankfulness, for it says:

My child, pay attention to what I say. Listen carefully to my words. Let them penetrate deep into your heart, for they bring life to those who find them, and healing to their whole body. Guard your heart above all else, for it determines the course of your life. Avoid perverse talk; stay away from corrupt speech. Look straight ahead and fix your eyes on what lies before you. Mark out a straight path for your feet; stay on the safe path. Don't get sidetracked; keep your feet from following evil.

Let us pray:
Dear Heavenly Father, thank you for granting me such favor, and assuring me that I need not be anxious for anything, Amen.

Verse 61

"For everything there is a season, a time for every activity under heaven." (Ecclesiastes 3:1)

Words for thought:

There is a reason for everything during our lifetime. The hardest part for us alcoholics is accepting life exactly how it is supposed to be. We played God with our lives, and of those among us, because we knew better, but we were wrong. Our judgment was fixated on how we would get our next drink, not on the good for ourselves or others. We pretended—well, hell, some of us functioned well—but in the end, it all crumbled. It came falling down because there was no sturdy foundation. We didn't listen when God spoke because we felt damaged and unredeemable. Be that as it may, at some point during our drunken stupors, we sat and pondered what it would be like to be sober and because of this, we were given the gift of desperation. In spite of the AA program, not all are as fortunate as we to receive the gift, and those unfortunate ones well, they remain drunk, while still others sadly pass from this earth dying from an alcoholic death. Nonetheless, the one thing we all have in common is God, for He is never changing and awaits patiently for *all* His children to come to Him in prayer. In fact, He says, "I am close to all who call on me, yes, to all who call on me in truth" (Psalm 145:18).

Let us pray:
Dear Heavenly Father, thank you because I know that all I have to do is believe in You with blind faith and you give me comfort in my time of need, Amen.

Verse 62

*"My child, don't lose sight of common sense and dis-
cernment. Hang onto them, for they will refresh your
soul…" (Proverbs 3:21-22)*

Words for thought:

We cannot forget the feelings of uselessness, self-pity, bitterness, resentment, anger, and fear, because this is where
our disease led our thinking. Day after day we drank, got drunk,
and passed out. We damaged family ties, friendships, careers.
All because we did not know that a power greater than ourselves
could restore us to sanity—that is, until that one final day of
great desperation we cried out and, on that day, a true miracle
occurred: we heard God. Thereafter, we had to ask ourselves
two important questions, and we had to make a choice. Do I
continue down this path of destructive drunken hell, or do I let
go and let God? Let's listen to what He says:

Trust in me with all your heart; do not depend on your own
understanding. Seek my will in all you do, and I will show
you which path to take. Don't be impressed with your own
wisdom. Instead, fear me and turn away from evil. Then you
will have healing for your body and strength for your bones.
(Proverbs 3:5-12)

Let us pray:
*Dear Heavenly Father, thank you for carrying me when the
storms were too great, Amen.*

Verse 63

*"But don't just listen to God's word. You must do what
it says. Otherwise, you are only fooling yourselves."
(James 1:22)*

Words for thought:

Within our lifetime there will be many mountains we must climb, and we will have incredible difficulties trying to climb them while living an alcoholic life. However, there is one who has all the power who will give us the strength to climb those mountains to live a life sober, but we must believe. We must believe in the power of God that, by one day at a time, He will give us guidance, wisdom, and truth. His Word says, "Joyful is the person who finds wisdom, the one who gains understanding …that wisdom will guide us down delightful paths; because all her ways are satisfying, and that wisdom is a tree of life to those of us that embrace her; and happy are those who hold on tightly" (Proverbs 3:13-18).

Let us pray:
*Dear Heavenly Father, thank you for granting me the wisdom
to know the difference, Amen.*

Verse 64

So letting your sinful nature control your mind leads to death. But letting the spirit control your mind leads to life and peace. For the sinful nature is always hostile to God. It never did obey God's laws, and it never will. That's why those who are still under the control of their sinful nature can never please God. (Romans 8:6-8)

Words for thought:

We must be aware of what we are thinking about. Our flesh tells us many lies, so we must be attentive in how we think. We need to watch for the dangers that alcohol places in our path because this evil is caused by Satan and he is slick. Remember He only comes to kill, steal, and destroy. He will come through people, places, and things just as our God does, but God brings us joy while Satan brings discord. The drink makes us think unclearly, but sobriety keeps us alert to God and His Word.

Let us pray:
Dear Heavenly Father, thank you that I get to enjoy a wonderful, peaceful life by keeping my thoughts aligned with your words, Amen.

Verse 65

"Seek the Kingdom of God above all else, and He will give you everything you need."(Luke 12:31)

Words for thought:

God knows our heart. He knows everything about our life beforehand because it has been written. Even without our asking, He shows us mercy, love, grace, and forgiveness, despite our character defects. We could not understand how God could love us because we consciously and unconsciously made the same mistakes over and over again due to our drinking. Saying we were sorry was no longer viable. It was changed behavior that we needed to achieve in our sobriety. Within the rooms of AA, God is prevalent. He is in our twelve steps. He is in our traditions. In fact, He is coming through loud and clear from every person that shares their victory of their very own recovery. Let us remember not to drink is our number one goal, but God is our top priority. There is nothing more important than Him in this world. So ask Him today for growth, wisdom, guidance, humility, and purpose and all these things will be added unto you.

Let us pray:
Dear Heavenly Father, thank you for loving me and giving me new a life to live sober, Amen.

Verse 66

"And I will ask the father, and He will give you another advocate to help you and be with you forever-the spirit of truth. The world cannot accept Him, because it neither sees Him or knows Him. But you know Him, for He lives with you and will be in you."
(John 14:16-17)

Words for thought:

Once we have made the glorious choice to put down the bottle, we begin to slowly grow in the spiritual realm of God. At first, there is going to be resistance because we laid for a long time with Satan. We allowed him to dictate our minds and emotions to the point of insanity, so trusting in God will not be an overnight matter, but a day to day victory. Only God can give us the spirit of truth and our will will be tested like a tug of war, and at times we will feel that we cannot win, but the truth of this matter is that God never gives us more than we can handle. Just look at the promise of 1 Corinthians 10:13: it says that the temptations in our life are no different from what others experience, and it continues to tell us God is faithful and that He will not allow temptation to be more than we can stand. So when we are tempted, He will show us a way out so that we can endure.

Let us pray:
Dear Heavenly Father, thank you for allowing me to lean on you in all my troubles, Amen.

Verse 67

"Do not be quickly provoked in your spirit, for anger
resides in the lap of fools." (Ecclesiastes 7:9)

Words for thought:

After achieving sometime in the program, we must be careful to never rest on our own laurels. We very much put ourselves at risk for a slip if we are to do so. We must never take our eyes off of God, for if we do, we will become unfocused. Then the shortcomings of anger, self-pity, and depression will set in, and it won't be long before we are drinking again. There is nothing we can get rid of on our own strength, so God must always come first. We are to commit our actions to the Lord, and all our plans will succeed (Proverbs 16:3). We should always have our eyes upward toward God so we do not quit before the miracle happens.

Let us pray:
Dear Heavenly Father, thank you for supplying me the strength
to stay close to you, Amen.

Verse 68

*"The soothing tongue is a tree of life, but a perverse
tongue crushes the spirit." (Proverbs 15:4)*

Words for thought:

I t is very much the truth that while we were drunk, it didn't
matter what came out of our mouth. A gentleman was no
longer a gentleman and a lady was no longer a lady. See, Satan
stayed busy assigning words that would cut others like a sword.
It is simply not true that "sticks and stones may break my bones
but words will never hurt me." The tongue has much power and
words hurt, so when we were complaining, gossiping, judging,
and criticizing with sarcasm dripping from our tongues, Satan
was laughing because He didn't care who we hurt. Do not let
Him win in sobriety. We come into the program and not only do
we get sober, but we clean up our act, and we regain the dignity
we lost. God says this: "A truly wise person uses few words;
a person with understanding is even-tempered. Even fools are
thought wise when they keep silent; with their mouths shut, they
seem intelligent" (Proverbs 17:27-28).

Let us pray:
*Dear Heavenly Father, thank you for the kind words I speak that
are acceptable to you, Amen.*

Verse 69

*"Therefore, as Gods chosen people, holy and dearly
loved, clothe yourselves with compassion, kindness,
humility, gentleness, and patience." (Colossians 3:12)*

Words for thought:

Sometimes we ask ourselves, "Why me? Why did God save
me?" We were a drunken mess who either lost everything
or we were on the verge of losing everything. But God's grace
saved us all. So why did He do this for us? Simply because He
loves us. We are no longer alone because He is here, alive and
living in us. And now that we know this, we no longer choose
to live in our sinful ways. We must go forward in God's comfort and His unchanging, steadfast ways and let others see Him
through us in all our ways.

Let us pray:
*Dear Heavenly Father, thank you for loving me. I will work on
what I find difficult to accept in myself today, Amen.*

Verse 70

"Wine produces mockers; alcohol leads to brawls. Those led astray by drink cannot be wise." (Proverbs 20:1)

Words for thought:

Steps ten, eleven, and twelve keep us moving in the solution one day at a time. Ten: once we take a personal inventory and see our misgivings, we promptly admit our wrongs. Eleven: we continuously seek God's love and approval through prayer and meditation. Twelve: we put our hand out to the next sick and suffering and practice all the principles in our affairs. These secure our seats in recovery. We never have to pick up another drink or drug if we simply display self-control, self-discipline, and total reliance upon God. Our spiritual self depends on it!

Let us pray:

Dear Heavenly Father, thank you for guiding me and being patient with me and allowing me to hear your Word, Amen.

Verse 71

"Let all bitterness and wrath and anger and clamor and slander be put away from you, along with all malice. Be kind to one another, tenderhearted, forgiving one another, as God in Christ forgave you." *(Ephesians 4:31-32)*

Words for thought:

As an alcoholic, there were so many feelings that kept us in the bottle: fear, resentment, bitterness, anger, dishonesty, self, self, self. However, putting down that first drink, we found something magnificent: God! We then learned to walk in His obedience and we allow His mercy, love, and freedom to guide us. One day at a time, we ask God to transform our mind so everything we do, think, and see is glorifying to Him. The Word tells us to throw off our old sinful nature and our former way of life because it is corrupted by lust and deception. We are to let the spirit renew our thoughts and attitudes. We are to put on our new nature which is created to be like God who is truly righteous and holy (Ephesians 4:2-24).

Let us Pray:
Dear Heavenly Father, thank you for arming me with the strength I need to follow the path you have offered me, Amen.

Verse 72

"People may be right in their own eyes, but the Lord examines their heart." (Proverbs 21:2)

Words for thought:

We cannot always prevent ourselves from having opinions, but we do have a choice to say, "It's none of my business." Sometimes we need to close our mouths and seek to listen more and understand instead of being understood. Alcohol clouded our thinking, our responses, and our reactions. At times, we made complete and utter fools of ourselves by our drunken point of view as we slurred, swaying and carrying on, and then we would be remorseful the next day not remembering what we said, but knowing it could not be good. But what we can say to this is thank God yesterday is gone, and a new day has dawned for us to say, "Father, forgive me for I have sinned against my fellows. Please help me to be sober-minded and to live, think, and act according to your Word."

Let us pray:
Dear Heavenly Father, thank you for cleansing my heart of things that do not reflect you, Amen.

Verse 73

"If you look for me wholeheartedly, you will find me."
(Jeremiah 29:3)

Words for thought:

E very day when we open our eyes, sober, is a day to give thanks and gratitude to our most high. It is of utmost importance to remember that it is only by God's grace that we no longer crave the drink and the insanity that it brings. We must never take credit for this gift of sobriety because it comes as a gift from our Father. When we surrender our will to Him, we enter into His presence and God becomes our refuge and shield against all things evil. His Word becomes our only source of hope.

Let us pray:
Dear Heavenly Father, thank you for allowing me peace in the midst of all my fears, Amen.

Verse 74

*"May the words of my mouth and the meditation of
my heart be pleasing to you, Lord." (Psalm 19:14)*

Words for thought:

We need to worship God with our words. When we choose
our words wisely, they will be uplifting and joyful. We spent
many years being loyal to Satan, saying whatever lustful lie
we could create to hide our alcoholism. We no longer need to
feel worthless, insecure with no value to our friends and family,
because we now know we have a new way to approach each
twenty-four hours. We can live in this world accepting every
person, place, and thing being exactly as it is, and not the way
we want it to be. Whenever we doubt, we turn to God's Word.
Just look at what 2 Timothy 3:16 encourages us. It tells us that
all Scripture is inspired by God and is useful to teach us what
is true and to make us realize what is wrong in our lives. It corrects us when we are wrong and teaches us to do what is right.

Let us pray:
*Dear Heavenly Father, thank you for helping me choose to med-
itate on your Word so when I speak, they are filled with kindness
and love, Amen.*

Verse 75

*"I will guide you along the best pathway for your life.
I will advise you and watch over you." (Psalm 32:8)*

Words for thought:

When we were drinking, we chose to keep moving left when God said to go right. Our ego knew better than anyone of how our life was to be lived. Our agony, pain, and suffering from alcoholism didn't affect our lives for sometimes years to come, but in the end, there was always that fork in the road, and the question was: which way do I choose? Psalm 37:5 answers this question for us, for it says: "Commit everything you do to the Lord. Trust Him, and He will help you." See, through life there are many avenues and each road is rocky, but the "easy way", "the alcoholic way", is treacherous. So when we ask God for direction, we must be still, and we must wait for His guidance because He is close to the brokenhearted and He rescues those whose spirits are crushed (Psalm 34:18).

Let us pray:
Dear Heavenly Father, thank you for my safe passageway. Where you lead, Lord, I will follow, Amen.

Verse 76

"The faithful love of the Lord never ends! His mercies never cease. Great is His Faithfulness; His mercies begin afresh each morning." (Lamentations 3:22-23)

Words for thought:

In our fellowship, we learn why we drink. We drink excessively and compulsively because we suffer from the disease of alcoholism. But our program offers us a great gift, and that is the knowledge that we never have to drink again, one day at a time. But who will save us from all this chaos we've created throughout the years? God, He will save us from ourselves! Our world was broken and God knows there was much suffering, but instead of Him turning His back on us, He said, "Come to me, all of you who are weary and carry heavy burdens, and I will give you rest" (Matthew 11:28). Hallelujah!

Let us pray:
Dear Heavenly Father, thank you for never leaving me alone, Amen.

Verse 77

"Stand your ground, putting on the belt of truth and the body armor of God's righteousness."
(Ephesians 6:14)

Words of thought:

Suffering is a reality of this world. Satan wants us to have temporary pleasures. He wants us to drink ourselves to death. He wants us to go through trials and tribulations. He wants us to stray from God. Yes, sometimes we feel alone. Yes, there may be days our hearts are broken. Yes, our finances may run low and we feel out of options. Yes, we are going to have days where we just want to drink again; however, we must remember that God's presence is always with us and we should not be shaken, for He is right by our side.

Let us pray:
Dear Heavenly Father, thank you for teaching me that my body rests in the safety of your arms, Amen.

Verse 78

*"Show me the right path, O Lord; point out the road
for me to follow. Lead me by your truth and teach me,
for you are the God who saves me. All day long I put
my hope in you." (Psalm 25:4-5)*

Words for thought:

We can begin our day by making all the plans we desire, but
it will always be the Lord who determines our steps. He is
the only one who has the authority over our life. He has offered
us a new life free from our alcoholism and we must focus our
mind and heart on Him. If we apply His Word and direction in
our lives, He will surely answer all our prayers, because God's
love is unfailing!

Let us pray:
*Dear Heavenly Father, thank you for giving me the strength and
comfort for all my days, Amen.*

Verse 79

"Commit everything you do to the Lord. Trust Him, and He will help you." (Psalm 37:5)

Words for thought:

We thought the end of our time was near by the time God saved us. We knew drinking was taking our health, our self-worth, our wealth, and most importantly, time away from our families. We also knew we were sick with a disease that is so powerful that it consumed our mind, will, and emotions, but somehow, God took our alcoholism and called upon us to walk a journey of faith with Him. He offered us a spiritual awakening to not drink one day at a time, but He knows that to just not drink isn't enough—we have to do our part. We must work our AA program and then pass on to others our experience, strength, and hope. God will inspire us through Scripture and through people what is false in our lives. He teaches us to do what is right if we are paying attention. When He calls us out of our comfort zone, we must be willing and ready to obey. God tells us in Scripture to "keep on asking, and you will receive what you ask for. Keep on seeking, and you will find. Keep on knocking and the door will be opened. For everyone who asks, receives. Everyone who seeks, finds. And to everyone who knocks, the door will be opened" (Luke 11:9-10). Hallelujah!

Let us pray:
Dear Heavenly Father, thank you for the many people you have placed in my life so I may share your good news, Amen.

Verse 80

"When people do not accept divine guidance, they run wild. But whoever obeys the law is joyful." (Proverbs 29:18)

Words for the day:

Coming into our recovery program, we were spiritually bankrupt. So when we read the second half of step two, "restore us to sanity," we began to get excited. Our lives had been so unmanaged for a long time due to our alcoholism, and God has been our solution all along! Now what we have to do next is in step three, and that is to acknowledge that God reigns! From there we relate to Him day by day through prayer and meditation to keep our faith strong. God reaches us every day by leaving clues and reminders all around us, but are we taking the time to slow down and notice?

Let us pray:
Dear Heavenly Father, thank you for having a path of recovery waiting for me, Amen.

Verse 81

"Have mercy on me, O God, according to your unfailing love; according to your great compassion blot out my transgressions." (Psalm 51:1)

Words for thought:

God wants us to go to Him in prayer and meditation for all things. His hands will gently guide us in the direction of untroubled waters. Although difficulties will arise, He will put His arms around us and shelter us from any harm. God brought us to a place in sobriety where He wants us to expect bigger things and He tells us to seek His kingdom above all else, and He will give us everything we need (Luke 12:31).

Let us pray:
Dear Heavenly Father, thank you for my safe place, and for your promise that you will meet me wherever I am, Amen.

Verse 82

*"The Lord leads with unfailing love and faithfulness
all who keep His covenant and obey His demands."
(Psalm 25:10)*

Words for thought:

I n our desperate time of need, God brought us to the doors of recovery. He then lead us one step at a time, one day at a time, to a place of serenity. We learned to trust that God's thoughts are high above our own thoughts, and that when we need His will, He is there to nudge us in the right direction. We must believe He knows what is best for our lives, because He has given us redemption, so if He closes one door, we wait and we pray, because another door shall open.

Let us pray:
Dear Heavenly Father, thank you for allowing thy will to be done here on Earth as it is in heaven, Amen.

Verse 83

"People who accept discipline are on the pathway to life, but those who ignore correction will go astray." (Proverbs 10:17)

Words for thought:

Each and every new day that dawns allows us to be in right standing with God, and through our fellowship, God gives us His grace; His beautiful and unmerited favor. We all came into recovery wanting to learn the reason why we drank, because we couldn't quite understand why we weren't like "normal drinking" people. What we discovered is that we drank excessively because we were alcoholics, and once we started, we had no defense against the next drink or the one after that. But we soon discovered that being sober teaches us how to live life on God's terms! God gives us the ability to think, speak, and act according to His Word. So, let's allow Him to discipline us, because only a fool hates discipline, and if we reject it, we are only harming ourselves, but if we listen to correction, we will grow in understanding (Proverbs 15:32).

Let us pray:
Dear Heavenly Father, thank you for the instructions you give me each new day, Amen.

Verse 84

"I will walk in freedom, for I have devoted myself to your commandments." (Psalm 119:45)

Words for thought:

Drinking and being drunk made us sloppy, ungrateful, immature, and in the end, we all reap what we sow! It is so important for us to think about what we are thinking about, because that forms a basis of what we do. We need to accept those unnecessary thoughts in our minds so those things do not define us, and we must not allow fear, shame, or doubt keep us from God. When we go to God, He will cleanse our heart. He is waiting to guide, assist, and redirect our "stinking thinking" today! So, the question is: are we ready for a change?

Let us pray:
Dear Heavenly Father, thank you for giving me your grace. I pray to stay in the here and now with you, Lord, Amen.

Verse 85

"Just as you cannot understand the path of the wind or the mystery of a tiny baby growing in its mother's womb, so you cannot understand the activity of God, who does all things." (Ecclesiastes 11:5)

Words for thought:

We have been made right in God's sight by faith. We took the step to believe that God is nothing or He is everything. This place we stand in is an undeserved privilege for we have all shown sin. However, through our fellowship, we discovered sorrow for those sins and we have been forgiven. So today, let our thoughts be centered on the Lord, for He is our refuge and our shield.

Let us pray:
Dear Heavenly Father, thank you for staying near me even though I have pushed you away, Amen.

Verse 86

"Therefore, as God's chosen people, Holy and dearly loved, clothe yourselves with compassion, kindness, humility, gentleness, and patience." (Colossians 3:12)

Words for thought:

H umility is a key ingredient to our success in our fellowship and recovery. We are to humble ourselves under the care of God and give to Him all our worries and cares. God promises to restore, support, and strengthen us, so we must start with our spiritual cornerstone and build our foundation on Him.

Let us pray:
Dear Heavenly Father, thank you for allowing me to humble myself, and to come before you, so I may be redeemed from my past, Amen.

Verse 87

"When you go through deep waters, I will be with you.
When you go through rivers of difficulty, you will not
drown." (Isaiah 43:2)

Words for thought:

We all come to that place in the river where we must cross. Just dipping our toes in the water is a beginning, but as our faith begins to grow, so does our trust in our God. He promises to guide us, lead us, and sometimes carry us, not only during the calm, but also through the storms. Whenever we doubt, no matter where we are, we pray and call upon God, because through the stillness He will hear our plea.

Let us pray:
Dear Heavenly Father, thank you for being everywhere
I go, Amen.

Verse 88

"When doubts filled my mind, your comfort gave me renewed hope and cheer." (Psalm 94:19)

Words for thought:

We need to keep God in our constant presence so we may commune with Him throughout our day. We do a spot check inventory during our twenty-four hours to be sure we are not full of self-will. God tells us that we are not obligated to do what our sinful nature tells us to do, however, at times, we have all fallen short of the glory of God, but He still chooses to forgive us our trespasses! God has created this wonderful sober life for us to live. A life free from alcohol; a life free of fear, worry, and doubt.

Let us pray:
Dear Heavenly Father, thank you for all of your glory, Amen.

Verse 89

"He leads the humble in doing right, teaching them His way." (Psalm 25:9)

Words for thought:

Put all your desires before God. Be confident that He will lead you to righteousness. Putting down the drink allowed God to restore us. He returned our souls to us refreshed and revitalized. Our insanity has been brought back to soundness of mind. Moment by moment, day by day, God has a great plan for us. We are to remain patient, loving, tolerant, and giving.

Let us pray:
Dear Heavenly Father, thank you for guiding me into doing the next right thing, Amen.

Verse 90

*"The Lord is my rock, my fortress, and my savior;
my God is my rock in whom I find protection. He is
my shield, the power that saves me, and my place of
safety." (Psalm 18:2)*

Words for thought:

Although we were lost and chained to our disease, hope came when we called God's name. He began teaching us how to handle the little things, the daily irritations. We stepped out of our comfort zone and allowed Him to help us with love, patience, and perspective. God and our fellowship teaches us how to be loving, kind, and tolerant people, not only with ourselves, but with our fellowman. It offers us the freedom to continually work on our sobriety through prayer and meditation so we become that person who walks with gratitude, honesty, faith, hope, courage, willingness, and perseverance.

Let us Pray:
Dear Heavenly Father, thank you for the joy you put in my heart, and may I always express to others the love I have for you, Amen.

Verse 91

"If only you would prepare your heart and lift up your hands to Him in prayer! Get rid of your sins, and leave all iniquity behind you. Then your face will brighten with innocence, You will be strong and free of fear." (Job 11:13-15)

Words for thought:

Sometimes we sit and wonder how all the pieces of our lives are going to come together. The tragedies, the disappointments, the sorrowful, the happy, the joyful. In these moments it is important to remember that God is in the middle of it all. We must allow Him to reveal to us where we resist Him the most, so we can surrender it all to Him, because without His grace we are doomed to an alcoholic death. So the question is, are we ready to have God move this mountain in our lives?

Let us pray:
Dear Heavenly Father, thank you for your grace that washes over me time and time again, Amen.

Verse 92

"Give your burdens to the Lord, and he will take care
of you. He will not permit the godly to slip and fall."
(Psalm 55:22)

Words for thought:

W e have been remade in the eyes of God. He brought us back from the depths of our alcoholism. He wants to break the grip Satan has on our shame, guilt, doubt, and fear. He wants to save us, but we ask ourselves, "Do I want saving?" We ask, "Can I accept that sometimes my pain and suffering is just part of the divine plan?" So we must let go, and let God. We trust Him to cleanse our heart of all the things that do not reflect Him.

Let us pray:
Dear Heavenly Father, thank you for being all knowing and all powerful, Amen.

Verse 93

"I have chosen the way of faithfulness; I have set my heart on your laws." (Psalm 119:30)

Words for thought:

God leads us in all our circumstances. Yes, that's right: in sobriety we learn that God guides us along with every person, place, and thing, so we must remember to speak of God often throughout our journey. We need to pay attention to God's Scripture so we may pass it along to our fellowman. God's character is in all of us, if we diligently stay in His Word, and that is simply by imitating what He would do in all situations. Take some time to think and ask yourself, "Am I putting God first in my life?"

Let us pray:
Dear Heavenly Father, thank you for directing and guiding my every footstep, Amen.

Verse 94

"If you love those who love you, what credit is that to you? Even sinners love those who love them." (Luke 6:32)

Words for thought:

God's greatest command: love. How impossible that seems, because in our drunkenness we felt unlovable, but because God loved us first, and He gave us His grace, we are able to mirror His ways on Earth. We are instructed to love those who do not love us, love those who irritate us or betray us and let's not forget to love those who gossip about us. God has chosen us to love people who are unlovable.

Let us pray:
Dear Heavenly Father, thank you for loving me and guiding my path when I feel as though I am stumbling, Amen.

Verse 95

"In His kindness God called you to share in His eternal glory by means of Christ Jesus. So after you have suffered a little while, He will restore, support, and strengthen you, and He will place you on a firm foundation." (1 Peter 5:10)

Words for thought:

Did you ever notice that God did for us what we could not do for ourselves? The Lord gives us a fellowship that offers simple rules for us to obey. The twelve steps and its principles are life-changers. Are you ready for a change? Our step one is that we just don't drink. Steps two and three we accept and believe God is everything or He is nothing. Steps four through seven we release all the fear, anger, bitterness, shame, guilt, and self-loathing. Steps eight and nine we make amends, we say we are sorry, and we move on. Steps ten through twelve we continue working on self and help the next sick and suffering.

Let us pray:
Dear Heavenly Father, thank you that it is your will to be done here on Earth, Amen.

Verse 96

"Hear my cry, O God, listen to my prayer."
(Psalm 61:1)

Words for thought:

Being grateful at the end of the day did not come easy for us alcoholics. We were so full of self and self-destruction, we couldn't see the problem right in front of us. Our addiction had us fooled and Satan sat easy in hell, because he held us in a firm, tight grasp of alcoholism. He is a master of discord. But God, God is the one to whom we need to pour our hearts out. He is the one who wants to love us and forgive us our trespasses. He wants to fill us with love, joy, peace, patience, kindness, goodness, gentleness, and self-control. So, we put the drink down and take a leap of faith that we can recover from a mindless disease. We start by becoming humble before God and showing a thankful heart that expresses our appreciation of Him. But remember, listening to God is our decision. God will not force us to choose His will, but He will do everything He can to encourage us to say yes to His.

Let us pray:
Dear Heavenly Father, thank you for giving me everything that is good, Amen.

Verse 97

"*Joyful is the person who finds wisdom, the one who gains understanding.*" *(Proverbs 3:13)*

Words for thought:

We must pray for wisdom to know the difference. God provides us with opportunities and they are gifts. He provides us with one another and sheds light for all. We must be careful not to invest too much time on things that mean very little. God will speak to us; we need only listen. Set priorities within your day so you may focus on what matters! Forget about the insignificant things that are not in God's plan.

Let us pray:
Dear Heavenly Father, thank you for the provisions of all things good in my life, Amen.

Verse 98

*"My eyes are always on the Lord, for He rescues me
from the traps of my enemies." (Psalm 25:15)*

Words for thought:

We have a choice to be disciplined or not. God gave us free
will. He does not wish suffering upon us, but we simply
must obey a few simple rules. God offers us forgiveness, guidance, mercy, wisdom, and strength. He tells us in Psalm 46:10
to just "be still and know that I am God." Look, one day, at
some point, we all had our spiritual awakening. We all knew
that we couldn't continue life the way we were: drunk. We had
an inkling there might be something better than just death. So
when the day came that God called upon us, we heard Him. We
simply had to accept that we are the blessed ones. We are called
to a higher purpose other than to just waste away. God promises
to be our shield, our protector, our defender, our guide, and our
everlasting rock. Do we want to go back to a drunken, stupor
place of hell?

Let us pray:
*Dear Heavenly Father, thank you for your everlasting word in
Scripture so I may lead a life full of your greatness, Amen.*

Verse 99

"As I learn your righteous regulations, I will thank you by living as I should! I will obey your decrees. Please don't give up on me!" (Psalm 119:7-8)

Words for thought:

An alcoholic mind is replaced by God's grace. The Big Book tells us over and over that we must be spiritually fit to remain sober. Every day, wherever we look, we can see, hear, and feel God's love for us. He has already promised us that when we seek Him, we will find Him. God always waits patiently for us and if we allow Him, He will detoxify our past. He wants to set us free from the bondage of self because our sickness kept us captive in our own minds for many, many years. God wants us to know that we do not have to shut the door completely on our past, because without lessons, there would be nothing learned. He will help us to remain sober, one day at a time, so we can go into the future with hope and gratitude. If we stay deeply devoted to God, He will supply all the guidance, wisdom, and strength we need and it is promised in Psalm 37:23 that our Lord will direct the steps of the godly because He delights in every detail of our lives!

Let us pray:
Dear Heavenly Father, thank you for saving me, Amen.

Verse 100

*"Lord, turn to me and be gracious to me, for I am
lonely and afflicted." (Psalm 25:16)*

Words for thought:

Our empty hearts are a cry for God. We find ourselves sometimes in that vast and empty space, almost as if we were lost.
The bottle couldn't solve it. But the awesome news is, God
can! He knows all our pain and He does not want us looking to
the future with fear, distress, or shame. In Colossians 3:5 God
is telling us to put to death the sinful earthly things that lurk
inside of us, for if we do, we will share in all His glory. All we
have to do is abstain from alcohol and He will graciously offer
us to live life one day at a time, free from the bondage of self.
And remember when we posture ourselves to God, He validates,
accepts, and forgives our sins. Hallelujah!

Let us pray:
*Dear Heavenly Father, thank you for being just a whisper
away, Amen.*

Verse 101

"All scripture is inspired by God and is useful to teach us what is true and to make us realize what is wrong in our lives. It corrects us when we are wrong and teaches us to do what is right." (2 Timothy 3:16)

Words for thought:

It's so wonderful how life can become beyond our wildest dreams. But on any given day life can change with a simple thought, an action, a reaction, a word, a phone call, text, or email, or perhaps a knock at the door. Life is uncertain, and while we were drowning our woes and sorrows in the bottom of the bottle, God was waiting for us. He has been waiting our whole lives to have a relationship with us, but we had to meet Him halfway. When we want His help, we ask, and keep faith because the Scripture of Matthew 7:7 encourages us to "keep on asking, and you will receive what you ask for. Keep on seeking, and you will find. Keep on knocking, and the door will be opened to you." God's love and words are unchanging, so let's find that quiet place with Him to absorb His Word, so we can love Him, praise Him, glorify Him, and thank Him!

Let us pray:
Dear Heavenly Father, thank you for giving me the power to be passionate about you, Amen.

Verse 102

"You have done many good things for me, Lord, just as you promised. I believe in your commands; now teach me good judgment and knowledge." (Psalm 119:65-66)

Words for thought:

We may stumble and go astray, and we will never be perfect, but we can thank God, for He meets us right where we are. We have an intimate and personal relationship with Him in sobriety. We learn that He protects us, He nurtures us, He strengthens us, and gives us hope, He sheds light on our path when we feel lost. We once had no hope and no purpose to envision our future without a drink. We remained focused only on ourselves, filling our thoughts with self-pity, self-hatred, and self-destruction. But one day, God spoke to us and we had a revelation. We knew it had to be God, but how could we be sure? Well, we are sure, because here we are: sober! Remember, God does not want perfection, He wants us to seek His kingdom above all else and He wants us to live righteously so He may give us everything we need (Matthew 6:33).

Let us pray:
Dear Heavenly Father, thank you that I do not have to be perfect in your eyes, Amen.

Verse 103

*"I have wandered away like a lost sheep; come and
find me, for I have not forgotten your commands."
(Psalm 119:176)*

Words for thought:

M any of us did not know that God created us in His own image
(Genesis 1:26-27). We did not know how to love ourselves
because of the torture we endured day in and day out as our
alcoholism took over our lives. We were not created by God to
feel worthless, insecure, confused or unloved. It was our illness
that made us believe we had no purpose or value in this life. But
the Lord declares to us in Jeremiah 29:11 that He has plans for
us, plans that will prosper us and not harm us, plans to give us
hope and a future. Let us not be disobedient to what God has
called us to do. He wants us sober, and He wants us to spread
His Word to the next sick and suffering fellow member. Let us
keep in mind that all blessings flow from our Father and in every
circumstance, every heartache, and every joy. Everything we
do, God works for our good. Hallelujah!

Let us pray:
*Dear Heavenly Father, thank you for being my everlasting
God, Amen.*

Verse 104

"Great is His faithfulness. His mercies begin afresh each morning." (Lamentations 3:23)

Words for thought:

God is our warmth and security. He will remain our shield against all evil. Lord today, we come to you with humble gratitude and we give thanks that you never judged, you never condemned, nor did you ever reject us. We were sick and suffering from a disease that attaches itself to us mentally, physically, and spiritually, but we are not meant to die an alcoholic death. Jesus tells us to lay our burdens, cares, and worries at His feet and AA says to admit we are powerless over alcohol and that our lives had become unmanageable. It is grand to know that if we attach our spirit to those two things, then we are guaranteed a life beyond our wildest dreams.

Let us pray:
Dear Heavenly Father, I thank you, I praise you, and I give all the glory to you, Amen.

Verse 105

"This is the day the Lord has made. We will rejoice and be glad in it." (Psalm 118:24)

Words for thought:

We can either speak positive, uplifting, and encouraging things into existence in our lives or we can produce negative, gloomy, and discouraging things into our lives. Our disease puts us in the face of temptation every single day. It has aligned itself with Satan to take everyone and everything away from us. It wants us isolated, stripped of self-worth and dignity, but remember, Jesus said, "Get behind me Satan" so we pray, "O Lord I will mimic you in every way." Hallelujah!

Let us pray:
Dear Heavenly Father, thank you for allowing me the freedom to choose your will, Amen.

Verse 106

"Because of our faith, Christ has brought us into this place of undeserved privilege where we now stand, and we confidently and joyfully look forward to sharing God's glory." (Romans 5:2)

Words for thought:

Eighty years ago, doctors were telling people who drank too much that they needed a total spiritual experience if they were to recover. Which means we get to begin our sober lives on the bottom alcohol created. Although it is a messy place to begin, AA and God offer us the way. Bill W. suggests we read the Big Book and we will find our solution. God says read Scripture and we will find peace in the midst of the chaos and He tells us this because God Himself is peace. He chose us to be His holy people. He loves and tells us to clothe ourselves with tenderhearted mercy, kindness, gentleness, and patience. He says to make allowances for each other's faults, and forgive anyone who offends us. Remember, the Lord forgave us, so we must forgive others. But above all this, He says, clothe yourselves with love, which binds us all together in perfect harmony (Colossians 3:12-14). Fellow members, we have the opportunity to live two lifetimes—one drunk and one sober. Admit, accept, surrender.

Let us pray:
Dear Heavenly Father, thank you for allowing the people who came before me sketch a pathway for my own recovery, Amen.

Verse 107

"For the kingdom of God is not a matter of what we eat or drink, but of living a life of goodness and peace and joy in the Holy Spirit." (Romans 14:17)

Words for thought:

In the past, we wandered around with an emptiness in our soul. We tried to fill this void with jobs, money, friends, cars, houses, clothing, alcohol, drugs. We became so distracted with these things that we lost sight of God. Then our fellowship suggests we change our person, places, and things. They tell us to become accountable to someone else. They tell us to reach our hand out to the next sick and suffering. Ask yourself: what am I doing for my addiction today?

Let us pray:
Dear Heavenly Father, thank you for protecting me from my own carelessness and self-destructive ways, Amen.

Verse 108

"Don't be selfish; don't try to impress others as better than yourselves. Don't look out only for your own interests, but take an interest in others, too."
(Philippians 2:3-4)

Words for thought:

I don't know if I'll ever know myself well enough that I do not have to look at others in some fault-finding way. Some shortcomings are so glaring, while others can be sneaky little defects. I have to have absolute belief in God and pray for His divine power to remove those flaws that are killing me. I want to display good fruit to my fellow man and not be a hypocrite. I pray to represent God with my actions, not only my words.

Let us pray:
Dear Heavenly Father, please help me to remember what a gift it is to sit with you in prayer and meditation, Amen.

Verse 109

"My soul be quiet before God, for from Him comes my hope." (Psalm 62:5)

Words for thought:

We come to believe that nothing can touch our mind, will, and emotions as long as we believe that God is our shield and armor. He is our fortress, our stronghold, our salvation, our strength, and our refuge when troubles come. He is big enough for us to put our drink problem in His hands and leave it there one day at a time, because God reigns above all things, and He is good. God is close to those who trust Him (Nahum 1:7). Let us stay the course of sobriety and accept there will be pain and suffering, but this too shall pass. Life will be difficult sober, but no matter what we are not alone, because the Lord goes before us and makes a way. Let us trust God's truth. Thy will be done!

Let us pray:
Dear Heavenly Father, thank you that I no longer live in condemnation, Amen.

Verse 110

*"Let your roots grow down into Him, and let your lives
be built on Him. Then your faith will grow in the truth
you were taught, and you will overflow with thankfulness." (Colossians 2:7)*

Words for thought:

We may love God with all our heart and strength, but do we share Him with others? We would do anything, go to any length, spend our last dime, on that person we love, so do we feel the same way toward our Lord? Are we so utterly in love and grateful to Him for our sobriety that we will obey all of His commands? Remembering the greatest of all: love. When we pray, we pray for God to relieve our alcoholism for today. We ask Him to help us follow His commands so we may be free from the bondage of self. We ask Him to give us the wisdom, so we may help others be empowered by His Word. God offers us a path to follow that is filled with love, joy, and peace, so when we come to the fork in the road where we have to choose A or B, we ask God to keep us grounded in His presence, so we may have the courage to continually follow the road to our recovery.

Let us pray:
Dear Heavenly Father, thank you for allowing me to build my foundation brick after brick upon you, Amen.

Verse 111

"For you have been called to live in freedom, but don't use your freedom to satisfy your sinful nature. Instead, use your freedom to serve one another. For the whole law can be summed up in this one command: Love your neighbor as yourself." (Galatians 5:13-14)

Words for thought:

In fellowship we are not to judge others. However, it is suggested we stick with the winners! God puts people in our path to learn something from and those lessons can be for a reason, a season, or a lifetime. Some people we share love, and some laughter, others tears, and still others sorrow and pain. Life and death are sometimes so surreal, but remember through all this, the one thing that remains the same is our God.

Let us pray:
Dear Heavenly Father, thank you for allowing me to live in a time of such freedom, Amen.

Verse 112

"The Lord is my strength and my shield; my heart trusts in Him, and He helps me. My heart leaps for joy, and with my song I praise Him." (Psalm 28:7)

Words for thought:

Each new day we can let go and let God. We give Him our sickness and we surrender it all to Him. It will take practice, patience, persistence, courage, and strength to walk the path of sobriety, but it is better than our alternative: a drunken mess.

Let us pray:
Dear Heavenly Father, thank you for the amazing work you do in my life. I give you all the glory, Amen.

Verse 113

*"You will call on me and come and pray to me and I
will listen to you. You will seek me and find me with
all your heart." (Jeremiah 29:12-13)*

Words for thought:

We have to be on guard as to where we are tempted to put our
trust: in God's kingdom or this unstable world. Our character defects tell us how we need to be more reliant on God, and
the more we learn to put our trust in Him, the closer He is in
our heart. As we begin to grow in the Word of God, our knowledge and understanding of His love for us will grow. We will
gain confidence and we will begin spreading His good news to
one another! We will prayerfully thank Him every day, with
our arms wide open, for His blessing that we are sober today
by His grace alone.

Let us pray:
*Dear Heavenly Father, thank you for the relationship I have
with you today, Amen.*

Verse 114

"With my whole heart have I sought you, inquiring for and of you and yearning for you; oh let me not wander or step aside from your commandments." (Psalm 119:10)

Words for thought:

For us alcoholics we had to accept that believing in God and being spiritually fit is the only way to remain sober. When we struggle we know that we are beginning to return to our old ways: fearful, worrisome, sinful, lazy, tormented. But our God is bigger than our illness, and when He stands for us, then no one can stand against Him. Every day, we need to set our eyes on God and be deeply devoted to prayer so we can receive His wisdom, guidance, and strength. Let's dare to ask God for abundant blessings on our lives. We are worth it, as long as we have the right attitude.

Let us pray:
Dear Heavenly Father, thank you for always being strong and bringing me back to your Word when I feel lost, Amen.

Verse 115

"We can rejoice, too, when we run into problems and trials, for we know that they help us develop endurance." (Romans 5:3)

Words for thought:

Every day we awaken is a day of new experiences with God. Our old self would be waiting impatiently for the clock to tick to the time when we thought it was okay to drink. But God intervened; He became our refuge and only hope from our alcoholism. We needed change from the same old thing so we humbled ourselves before God. We joined a recovery program and we became confident, grateful, and transformed by the hand of God. Remembering, "it only works if we work it!"

Let us pray:
Dear Heavenly Father, thank you for your greatness and your blessings over us, Amen.

Verse 116

"For those who find me (wisdom) find life and receive favor from the Lord. But those who fail me (wisdom) harm themselves." (Proverbs 8:35-36)

Words for thought:

There are so many times we tried to hide our sins from God. After all, who wants to face their shortcomings. The defects weighed heavily upon the alcoholic's mind, will, and emotions. We kept falling short of our true selves. We tried so many times to fix ourselves, and failed. But there is a God who can put us on a healing path of recovery, if we so choose. A psalm of David clearly states, "the Lord directs the steps of the godly. He delights in every detail of their lives. Though they stumble, they will never fall, for the lord holds them by the hand" (Psalm 37:23-24). Every detail of our life must be turned over to the care of God so He may use us. He wants us to stop thinking so much about ourselves and to focus on others. Others that need our hand of hope because it is said, "I am responsible when anyone, anywhere, reaches out for help, I want the hand of AA always to be there. And for that; I am responsible."

Let us pray:
Dear Heavenly Father, thank you that I no longer have to live in the shadows of my addiction, Amen.

Verse 117

"Don't worry about anything; instead pray about everything. Tell God what you need, and thank Him for all He has done." (Philippians 4:6)

Words for thought:

I t is true we become what we think, so we must not think negatively, fearfully, or boastfully. Every day, we battle negative thoughts because alcohol convinced us that it was our friend, but it turned against us and became our worst enemy. It made us think bitterly and resentfully, and the deeper we allowed these to take root, the further we were from healing. See, these things are spiritual battles and only God can help us. Only He can take away our desire to drink. God has given us insight, so let's keep the fire burning in a relationship with Him, because He is an awesome God and He answers our prayers!

Let us pray:
Dear Heavenly Father, thank you for always being here for me in my times of troubles, Amen.

Verse 118

"Be careful for nothing; but in everything by prayer with thanksgiving let your requests be made known to God." (Philippians 4:6)

Words for thought:

For some, we considered our time was coming to an end. We just could not continue life drunk anymore. The very thing, alcohol, in which we thought was our solution, betrayed us and sank us to a level equal to Satan. It took our jobs, money, home, relationships, and made us feel isolated from all the good God has to offer. But guess what? We can still be thankful, because God uses sinful people such as ourselves every day. He will use us to become sober just so we can help the next sick and suffering. That's the key: one alcoholic talking to another. So however broken our lives may feel, we are to gather faith, because God is doing something great in our lives!

Let us pray:
Dear Heavenly Father, I thank you for my life and everything you have bestowed upon me, Amen.

Verse 119

"In the beginning the word already existed. The word was with God, and the word was God." (John 1:1)

Words for thought:

We all have a road to follow and the one we were on was stuck in the past, fueled by alcohol, that lead us to griping and complaining, asking ourselves how we got here again. We must be ever-diligent on our path with God, because His narrow road will lead to heaven and the other road, which is much wider, will lead us to hell. One pathway leads to alcohol while the other to sobriety. Fellow members, Satan preys on us. He has a plan for us, so we are to stay alert, because although His plan appears to be filled with beauty, it truly is just a disguise. May we, for today, choose our journey with God and live His holy word.

Let us pray:
Dear Heavenly Father, thank you for the pathway you have carved out for my new life, Amen.

Verse 120

"I prayed to the Lord, and He answered me. He freed me from all my fears." (Psalm 34:4)

Words for thought:

Has God called you to walk through something that may frighten you? Do you feel unsafe and uncertain? Is fear and anxiety rearing its ugly head? No worries; grab tightly to your trust in God and never give up because He cares about you. He loves you; He will carry you through your troubles. Let us live to love as God loves us, and let us bear witness to 1 Corinthians 13:4-7 because it tells of where our heart belongs:

Love is patient and kind. Love is not jealous or boastful or proud or rude. It does not demand its own way, it is not irritable, and it keeps no record of being wronged. It does not rejoice about injustice but rejoices whenever the truth wins out. Love never gives up, never loses faith, is always hopeful, and endures through every circumstance.

Let us pray:
Dear Heavenly Father, thank you for the new direction and guidance over my life today, Amen.

Verse 121

"Most important of all, continue to show deep love
for each other, for love covers a multitude of sins."
(1 Peter 4:8)

Words for thought:

When we brought ourselves to God and asked for forgiveness, He began to renew our souls. He lifted us up and out of our alcoholism and gave us His Word to learn to live by. God is all knowing in knowledge and wisdom so we seek from Him everything: hope, faith, growth, guidance, truth, happiness, and love. We must trust God's will for our lives because it is written: "Thy will be done in Earth as it is in heaven" (Matthew 6:10). The enemy will try to steal all our joy from the Lord; He is a liar and deceiver and He doesn't want that drink away from our hands, because He rejoices when we pursue the things that keep us farther and farther away from God. But remember the powerful love of God wins over the enemies lies because the Lord our God is a "God of compassion and mercy, He is slow to get angry and is filled with unfailing love and faithfulness" (Psalm 86:15).

Let us pray:
Dear Heavenly Father, thank you for the serenity that is in my life today because of your Word, Amen.

Verse 122

"Don't copy the behavior and customs of this world, but let God transform you into a new person by changing the way you think. Then you will learn to know God's will for you, which is good and pleasing and perfect." (Romans 12:2)

Words for thought:

It's a brand-new day. A fresh twenty-four hours! How are you going to live it: drunk or sober? Will you show love and tolerance to those in need? Will you share God's Word openly to another? Will you sit and meditate and give thanks for all He has done? Will you reject any toxic thoughts from Satan and replace them with God's Word? Will you be encouraging today and build others up? Do you want to be close to God today? This is what He says in Luke 9:23: "If any of you wants to be my follower, you must give up your own way, take up your cross daily, and follow me." Hallelujah!

Let us pray:
Dear Heavenly Father, thank you for being here to give me guidance when I have more questions than answers, Amen.

Verse 123

"But the fruit of the spirit is love, joy, peace, patience, kindness, goodness, gentleness and self-control. Against such things there is no law. Those who belong to Christ Jesus have crucified the flesh with its passions and desires. Since we live by the spirit, let us keep in step with the spirit." (Galatians 5:22-25)

Words for thought:

In our fellowship we are to lead by good example, honestly and humbly. We should not think highly of ourselves. We should not speak negatively against ourselves or others. We should never compare, but always identify. Let us allow God to flow through us toward others with love, confidence, thankfulness, and faithfulness. God loves us and tells us in Isaiah 41:10: "Fear not, for I am with you; be not dismayed, for I am your God; I will strengthen you, I will help you, I will uphold you with my righteous right hand."

Let us pray:
Dear Heavenly Father, thank you for the Lord Jesus, your one and only son, who sacrificed His life on the cross for me, Amen.

Verse 124

"Think about things of heaven, not the things of earth."
(Colossians 3:2)

Words for thought:

W hen too many negative thoughts dominated our mind, we searched for a drink to make it all better. We conformed to the evil of this world. We believed Satan's lies that we could have just one, but He is a liar. We know of his deceitful ways because Scripture tells us to be alert, and to be of sober mind and be vigilant, because our adversary, the devil, walks about like a roaring lion, seeking whom He may devour (1 Peter 5:8). The Lord is our Savior. He will help us stay away from that drink one day at a time. He will renew our mind with things beyond our wildest dreams. So let us not quit before the miracle happens.

Let us pray:
Dear Heavenly Father, thank you for saving my soul with your word, Amen.

Verse 125

"Don't be misled-you cannot mock the justice of God. You will always harvest what you plant. Those who live only to satisfy their own sinful nature will harvest decay and death from that sinful nature. But those who live to please the Spirit will harvest everlasting life from the Spirit." (Galatians 6:7-8)

Words for thought:

Upon awakening, we were already thinking about our next drink. This thought consumed our thinking until we took that first sip of the day. After a while, we were stumbling around four walls, banging our heads against them, wondering how we ever got this drunk again. We had just promised ourselves "no more," but here we were: slurring, sloppy, and inebriated. Satan had us eating out of His hands while He assisted us in complete self-destruction. But one day God made us strong enough to look in the mirror and examine ourselves and our actions. He gave us a way out, a solution to our drinking. He tells us we should pay careful attention to our own work, and not to compare ourselves to anyone else (Galatians 6:4). So let our first focus of the day be on God and His will for us, because only He can deliver us from our prison of alcoholism.

Let us pray:
Dear Heavenly Father, thank you for lifting me higher than my addiction, Amen.

Verse 126

"Don't you see how wonderfully kind, tolerant, and patient God is with you? Does this mean nothing to you? Can't you see that His kindness is intended to turn you from your sin." (Romans 2:4)

Words for thought:

When we decided to put the drink down and make the decision to trust in God for our sobriety, great things began to happen. We were slowly able to clear our minds of all the hurt and pain we caused ourselves and others. After a while, we began to see the many promises from the Big Book coming to pass in our daily lives. Things like, "We are going to know a new freedom and a new happiness," and, "We will comprehend the word serenity and we will know peace," and, "We will suddenly realize that God is doing for us what we could not do for ourselves" are all promises that will "materialize if we work for them." We are given tools for growth in AA, and if we use them, our character will become more like God. Remember, God is always first. Hallelujah!

Let us pray:

Dear Heavenly Father, thank you for the many promises you have fulfilled in my life, Amen.

Verse 127

"My child, pay attention to what I say. Listen carefully to my words. Don't lose sight of them. Let them penetrate deep into your heart, for they bring life to those who find them, and healing to their whole body." (Proverbs 4:20-22)

Words for thought:

God's Word tells us we must never follow the desires of our sinful nature. These sins include drunkenness, envy, hostility, selfish ambition, jealousy, and lustful pleasures. While intoxicated, we were living in Satan's den, allowing him to dictate to us and whisper temptations into our ears. See, our battle is not physical, it is spiritual, and only God Himself can save us from Satan's snare. So let us not drown our sorrows in booze by living depressed or anxious, but by renewing our minds with God's Word, remembering that His tools of faith, love, Scripture, and prayer will always give us our daily reprieve.

Let us pray:
Dear Heavenly Father, thank you for blessing me with the gift of sobriety. Amen.

Verse 128

"How great is our Lord! His power is absolute! His understanding is beyond comprehension! The Lord supports the humble, but He brings the wicked down into dust." (Psalm 147:5-6)

Words for thought:

Leave in God's hands the present and the future, knowing only that He is good. He can bring order out of chaos, good out of evil, and peace out of turmoil. God will turn our mess of alcoholism into a message that we can share with others who suffer just as we did. Our experience, strength, and hope to the newcomer will allow them to see that they are not alone. We can share with others all about the influence God has had over our spiritual life since becoming sober, so they may be able to feel the hope that we have gained while working our program.

Let us pray:
Dear Heavenly Father, thank you for giving me a brand-new direction for my life, Amen.

Verse 129

"I will bless the Lord at all times; His praise shall continually be in my mouth." (Psalm 34:1)

Words for thought:

All of God's work is done in faithfulness. Our temptation to sin (drink) never dies, and Satan will continually nip at our heels, so we must stay vigilant in our prayers. Once we are filled with the Holy Spirit, it encourages us to wait on God, and pray to Him about everything. God wants us to petition Him and tell Him what is in our heart today. When we feel overburdened with the taunting of evil, we can ask God to refresh our soul, because He promises that He is leaving us with a gift of peace of mind and heart, and the peace He gives us is a gift the world cannot give. So don't be troubled or afraid (John 14:27).

Let us pray:
Dear Heavenly Father, thank you for giving me peace of mind to get through my day, Amen.

Verse 130

So be careful how you live. Don't live like fools, but like those who are wise. Make the most of every opportunity in these evil days. Don't act thoughtlessly, but understand what the Lord wants you to do. Don't be drunk with wine, because that will ruin your life. Instead be filled with the Holy Spirit. (Ephesians 5:15-18)

Words for thought:

Do you know God wants us to believe in Him as much as He believes in us? He wants to do more for us than we can imagine. But He cannot do it until we ask, because He gives us free will to do with it what we want. So when the time arrived when we were "sick and tired of being sick and tired," God was waiting patiently for us to surrender, and one day at a time we learned how to live a sober life without alcohol—a life free of chaos, resentments, fear, misery, and self-torture. This is the place of peace we desire. As we slowly learn God's Word, and what it means to be His child, our hearts will overflow with gratitude. We will suddenly realize God is doing for us that which we could not do for ourselves. Friends, let us think about this: God has saved us from a horrible alcoholic death. He gave us a blueprint for living life, and He has allowed us to live two lifetimes: one drunk and one sober. Hallelujah!

Let us pray:
Dear Heavenly Father, thank you for saving me from myself, Amen.

Verse 131

"The Lord says I will rescue those who love me. I will protect those who trust in my name." (Psalm 91:14)

Words for thought:

S atan wants to distract us. He wants to keep us as drunk as the day before, because he is interested in blindsiding us. His evil lurks everywhere. He knows our habits, our weaknesses, even our deepest fears. But guess who else knows our heart? God, and the Word says that we are to put on every piece of God's armor so we will be able to resist the enemy in the time of evil. Then after the battle, we will be standing firm (Ephesians 6:13).

Let us pray:
Dear Heavenly Father, thank you for saving me from the darkness of evil, Amen.

Verse 132

"Fear of the Lord is the foundation of true knowledge, but fools despise wisdom and discipline."
(Proverbs 1:7)

Words for thought:

When we are fighting against some person, place, or thing, it is because we have not filtered the problem with God. When we are fighting against our own will not to drink it is because we have not given our life and will over to the care of God. We made a choice while drinking to live in our own flesh and not the Holy Spirit, but just putting down the drink is not enough. We need to renew our minds with a complete spiritual experience and ask God to create in us a clean heart. When we lack wisdom, we are to ask God, because He will generously give it to us without finding any fault with us. Remember, God's Word is full of wisdom and He awaits the time to bestow it upon us. James 3:17 explains wisdom from above is pure. It is also peace-loving, gentle at all times, and willing to yield to others. It is full of mercy and the fruit of good deeds. It shows no favoritism and is always sincere.

Let us pray:
Dear Heavenly Father, thank you for allowing me the wisdom to know the difference, Amen.

Verse 133

"Trust in the Lord with all your heart; do not depend on your own understanding. Seek His will in all you do, and He will show you which path to take." (Proverbs 3:5-6)

Words for thought:

We, who are believers in God, need to be open to receive His love. Knowing His Word requires us to give time and energy to Him daily. We need to be listening and we need to be willing to discover His deep love for us. God reveals Himself to us as we believe.

Let us pray:
Dear Heavenly Father, thank you for accepting my prayers that I ask of you, Amen.

Verse 134

Who has anguish? Who has sorrow? Who is always fighting? Who is always complaining, who has unnecessary bruises? Who has bloodshot eyes? It is the one who spends long hours in the taverns, trying out new drinks. Don't gaze at the wine, seeing how red it is, how it sparkles in the cup, how smoothly it goes down. For in the end it bites like a poisonous snake; it stings like a viper. You will see hallucinations, and you will say crazy things. You will stagger like a sailor tossed at sea, clinging to a swaying mast. And you will say they hit me, but I didn't feel it. I didn't even know when they beat me up. When will I wake up so I can look for another drink? (Proverbs 23:29-35)

Words for thought:

God knew long before us that someday we would need to return to Him with a broken spirit. Our falling down drunkenness no longer worked for us and we needed divine intervention. He gave us fellowship and others to help us with our disease. We never have to be alone again. Remember, "the Lord Himself will fight for you. Just stay calm" (Exodus 14:14).

Let us pray:
Dear Heavenly Father, thank you for clearing a path for me in sobriety, Amen.

Verse 135

"You were like sheep going astray, but now you have returned to the shepherd and overseer of your souls."
(1 Peter 2:25)

Words for thought:

How did we get so lost and not know where to go? We went to the bottom of the bottle and discovered we couldn't climb out alone. We drank to get drunk and then started it all over again the next day. We lived in the insanity day after day, playing on the merry-go-round that kept us spinning out of control. Our attitudes, emotions, and speech were thwarted from growing in God's Word because we were in bed with Satan. We did not believe we could be saved, because we strayed from God's sight from our guilt, shame, and ego. But one day, suddenly, we found that although we did not remain loyal to God, He remained loyal to us and we quickly learned, "God is our refuge and strength, always ready to help in times of trouble" (Psalm 46:1).

Let us pray:
Dear Heavenly Father, thank you for lifting me above my troubles, at just the right time, Amen.

Verse 136

*"Let all bitterness and indignation and wrath, and
resentment and quarreling and slander be banished
from you. And become useful and helpful and kind
to one another, tenderhearted, forgiving one another,
as God in Christ forgave you." (Ephesians 4:31-32)*

Words for thought:

We all came into a fellowship the same way: beaten, broken,
and defeated. Slowly, one day at a time, we learned to live
life on God's terms. We were given a gift in the twelve steps and
slowly, in working them, we learn to let go and let God. God
tells us to get rid of all evil behavior. He says to be done with
all deceit, hypocrisy, jealousy, and unkind speech. He wants
us to be like newborn babies, who crave pure milk so we may
grow into a full experience of salvation. He wants us to cry out
for this nourishment now that we have had a taste of His kindness (1 Peter 2:2-3).

Let us pray:
*Dear Heavenly Father, thank you for giving me a reason to live
life again, Amen.*

Verse 137

"Trust in the Lord with all your heart; do not depend on your own understanding." (Proverbs 3:5)

Words for thought:

We should always consult God above all else. He leaves us signs along our journey and it is up to us to be obedient to follow His instructions. God tells us to be anxious for nothing because He is guarding our way. Stay on course, shielding all evil with God's Word, and we shall experience His fruits.

Let us pray:
Dear Heavenly Father, thank you that when I steer off course you are there to guide me, Amen.

Verse 138

"He will not let you stumble; the one who watches over you will not slumber." (Psalm 121:3)

Words for thought:

Everything has an expiration date, thank you God! Can you imagine if our drinking days did not expire? God has a promise of blessings if we listen to His instructions and discipline ourselves in His Word. He promises to keep us from all harm while He watches over our life. He will keep watch over us as we come and go, both now and forever (Psalm 121:8). God gives us great hope for our future, so we do not have to invite all the insanity back into our lives by picking up that first drink, because our powerless struggle and insanity stops with God.

Let us pray:
Dear Heavenly Father, thank you that I no longer have to suffer, Amen.

Verse 139

"My child pay attention to what I say. Listen carefully to my words." (Proverbs 4:20)

Words for thought:

We were all once held captive by Satan's trap. We listened to his foolish and godless ways. Every time we put a sip of liquor to our lips, we showed godless behavior. However, there came a day when God whispered in our ear the error of our ways. He saved us from a living hell. Our soul no longer hurt from the drink. God wants us to avoid worthless temptations and to continue to turn away from evil because His truth stands firm; He is our foundation and His Word tells us that His faithful love never ends and that His mercies never cease. How great is God's faithfulness, because His mercies begin afresh each morning! Let us repeat, "The Lord is my inheritance; therefore, I will hope in Him" (Lamentations 3:22-24).

Let us pray:
Dear Heavenly Father, thank you for being my rock and redeemer, Amen.

Verse 140

"No discipline is enjoyable while it is happening - it's painful! But afterward there will be a peaceful harvest of right living for those who are trained in this way." (Hebrews 12:11)

Words for thought:

We began at an early age in life seeking love, purpose, and meaning. Some folks were met with these basic needs early on, while others ran as far away from them as possible, because of some sort of tragedy, neglect, or self-inflicted pain. And what we alcoholics did was run as far away from God as possible, directly to the bottle. There was nothing that could fill the void. No amount of alcohol, no geographical change, and no human aid could save us. We hit our alcoholic bottom. But when we hit our absolute lowest, that's when we heard God. We prayed, "Dear God, please take this from me. I can no longer live in this sin. I can no longer deny my disease. My character defects are killing me, please remove them, I am sorry. Please help me." Now, it is up to us, one day at a time, to do as the disciples did when Jesus said, "Follow me."

Let us pray:
Dear Heavenly Father, thank you for the gift of purpose, Amen.

Verse 141

"But people who aren't spiritual can't receive these truths from God's Spirit. It all sounds foolish to them and they can't understand it, for only those who are spiritual can understand what the spirit means." (1 Corinthians 2:14)

Words for thought:

One day we came to the realization that we chose the life we live. Once we sobered up long enough, we learned our disease is like an "allergy" and once we began drinking, we had no willpower to fend off the next. Our obsession and compulsion had just won and here we were, drunk, once again. Then, one day it was suggested we lean on a power greater than ourselves, God. We learned He could restore us to sanity when we turn our will and our lives over to His care. Some may think there is a better way, but there is not. There is a void in us that needs filling and it is God's Word that fills that void, so it is spirituality we must seek to remain of sober mind. Read what God's Word in Romans 6:20-22 conveys to us:

When you were slaves to sin, you were free from the obligation to do right. And what was the result? You are now ashamed of the things you used to do, things that end in eternal doom. But now you are free from the power of sin and have become slaves of God. Now you do those things that lead to holiness and result in eternal life.

Let us pray:
Dear Heavenly Father, thank you for this day and may it be filled with your will and not my own, Amen.

Verse 142

*"Those who love your instructions have great peace
and do not stumble. I long for your rescue, Lord, so
I have obeyed your commands. I have obeyed your
laws, for I love them very much. Yes, I obey your commandments and laws because you know everything I
do." (Psalm 119:165-168)*

Words for thought:

It is important for us not to become lazy, passive, or complacent
about our spiritual condition. Obedience to God requires work
on our part every single day. We must stay motivated as we
continue to grow in His love, wisdom, and knowledge because
we are called to be God's children. But we are not called to
love this world nor the things it offers us, for when we love the
world, then we do not have the love of the Father in us. The
world only offers a craving for physical pleasure, a craving for
everything we see, and pride in our achievements and possessions. See, these things are not from the Father, but from this
world. This world is fading away, along with everything that
people crave. But anyone who does what pleases God will live
forever (1 John 2:15-17).

Let us pray:
*Dear Heavenly Father, thank for your nourishing instructions
that you provide for me, Amen.*

Verse 143

"So be strong and courageous, all you who put your hope in the Lord!" (Psalm 31:24)

Words for thought:

God will give us the strength and direction to do the right thing no matter what the circumstances. In the morning, we ask Him to free us of self so we may be of service to others. Throughout our day, we continuously commune with Him before we take any action, especially if that action may force us to drink. We alcoholics have been given a new life through God's Word. He has prepared a new heart for us. One that will be quick to listen, slow to speak, and slow to get angry (James 1:19). But we must do our part: abstinence, fellowship, forgiveness, and love.

Let us pray:
Dear Heavenly Father, thank you for your goodness and blessings over my life, Amen.

Verse 144

*"And let the peace that comes from Christ rule in
your hearts. For as members of one body you are
called to live in peace and always be thankful."
(Colossians 3:15)*

Words for thought:

The important question to ask ourselves upon awakening is if
God is our closest friend. He created a miracle for us when He
brought us into a world of sobriety. He knew we were not alone in
our suffering, so He gave us fellowship. He said, "Go share your
experience, strength, and hope to the next sick and suffering alcoholic." God does not want us to regret our past, but to learn from
it. He wants to give us the wisdom to make our decisions based
on what will make us happy later. We suffered far too long with
frustration, ego, anxiety, and resentment. We were unloving, harsh,
and angry. We lashed out at those who love us the most, because
we were too drunk to rationalize right from wrong. Ecclesiastes
7:9 tells us to "control our temper, for anger labels us a fool," but
we just could not stop. Our self-will was powerful and we let Satan
rule our desires, because he will do anything to keep us from our
Father, until that one day when God saved our life. That one day
when God said we have only been called to be in this world, but
not of it and all its evil ways. So remember, we must live one
minute at a time, one hour at a time, and one day at a time, without
putting a drink to our lips. Hallelujah!

Let us pray:
*Dear Heavenly Father, thank you for helping me to set my eyes
and my heart on you, Amen.*

Verse 145

"Lord, you are mine! I promise to obey your words!
With all my heart I want your blessings. Be merciful
as you promised." (Psalm 119:57-58)

Words for thought:

We must seek God to feel good about ourselves. When we
seek the alcohol, we are seeking something temporary to
rid ourselves of feelings, and therefore we are replacing a cheap
substitute in place of our God. We used the alcohol to make
us feel like we were on top of the world, but that top began to
crumble with our sinful thoughts and our desire to drink. Our
time turned into meaningless days, nights, weeks—even years.
Our pride filled us with rebellion, lies, unrealistic views, and
poor judgment. Our pain, suffering, and misery brought about
much torment, and we did not know if we could live one more
day with our lazy, grumbling, complaining, drunken selves.
Thankfully, due to God's perfect will, He bestowed upon us
grace and mercy, and we have been saved. God's everlasting
eternal love gives us guidance, forgiveness, discipline, and salvation, and as we learn His righteous regulations, we will live as
we should and obey His decrees while pleading, "Lord, please
do not give up on me!" (Psalm 119:7-8)

Let us pray:
Dear Heavenly Father, thank you for loving me just the way I
am, Amen.

Verse 146

"Oh the joys of those who do not follow the advice of
the wicked, or stand around with the sinners, or join
in with mockers. But they delight in the law of the
Lord, meditating on it day and night." (Psalm 1:1-2)

Words for thought:

I t used to be when we were alone and isolated, we thought we were fine. We didn't need anybody because our best friend, liquor, was all we wanted and needed. Yet, our minds became tortured by the feelings of uselessness, self-pity, hatred, and resentments. No matter how many hands our family and friends reached out to us, we denied their help, and no matter how many times God prompted us, we couldn't or wouldn't listen. So we kept falling deeper and deeper to the bottom of existence until we reached our end, and at some point, we all reach an end during our active addiction. Some results are similar, while others may be different, but we all get there no matter the differences. See, liquor doesn't discriminate; it comes after us young, middle-aged, or old. However, what we all do have in common is we recover the same way: through fellowship, abstinence, one day at a time, and by God's grace.

Let us pray:
Dear Heavenly Father, thank you for being here for me today! Amen.

Verse 147

"But seek ye first the kingdom of God, and His righteousness, and all these things shall be added unto you." (Matthew 6:33)

Words for thought:

We have to be ready and willing to invite God into our hearts, for He is waiting. Continue to be vigilant in prayer and discipline and wait for all the good things that will happen. Things may not come immediately, but if it is God's will, they will come. Remember: "Don't quit before the miracle happens."

Let us pray:
Dear Heavenly Father, thank you for waiting for me to come to your will, Amen.

Verse 148

"My child, listen to what I say, and treasure my commands. Tune your ears to wisdom, and concentrate on understanding. Cry out for insight, and ask for understanding." (Proverbs 2:1-3)

Words for thought:

It takes time and discipline for us to become God's servant. Disobedience to His Word does not only hurt us; it hurts Him. The enemy knows what we are thinking and what we are taught, so let's be vigilant in prayer. God's Word teaches us many things, but love and tolerance is what we need in our time of recovery. We come to God because He is a prayer-answering God. We submit to Him our brokenness, alcoholism, and all our sins and we humbly go to Him for repentance.

Let us pray:
Dear Heavenly Father, thank you for reminding me that it is not all about me, but about your word, Amen.

Verse 149

*"Dear children, let us not love with words or speech
but with actions and truth." (1 John 3:18)*

Words for thought:

We all need a guide in life and what better adviser than our Lord, God. Today we need to take time and thank Him for the beautiful gift of sobriety. Also thanking Him for the family, friends, and fellow members He places on our beaten path. We were lost, sick, and tired of the insanity of drinking, so we prayed, and God brought us to a place of wholeness. He took all our broken pieces and fit them back into a solid foundation on which we could stand. While recovering, we just continued doing the next right thing day after day and before our eyes, a change came about us. Sometimes the change was quick, sometimes slow, but we were able to do it all sober!

Let us pray:
Dear Heavenly Father, thank you for the gift of life, Amen.

Verse 150

"Give all your worries and cares to God, for He cares about you." (1 Peter 5:7)

Words for thought:

sn't it wonderful that we need not think about tomorrow, because tomorrow will bring thoughts all of itself? God has given us this perfect day to rejoice and be glad in it, and our present day without alcohol is purely a given gift from God. We do all the work, but God receives all the glory. His Word in 1 Peter 3:11 tells us to "turn away from evil and do good. Search for peace, and work to maintain it" remembering that "just as the body is dead without breath, so also faith is dead without good works" (James 2:26).

Let us pray:
Dear Heavenly Father, thank you for the courage, strength, and hope you have provided me with today, Amen.

Verse 151

"The teaching of your word gives light, so even the simple can understand." (Psalm 119:130)

Words for thought:

Sometimes in life, our day will be going so well and our gratitude is at an all-time high. We are sober and celebrating our new relationship with God, but then something unexpected occurs and it stops us dead in our tracks. What are we supposed to do? We cannot drink—that is what we use to do. But our new self will put away any fears, we will pray, and use the tools from our program. We will draw on the Word of God, because His instructions, from Genesis to Revelation, bring us His love and it gives us His peace.

Let us pray:
Dear Heavenly Father, thank you for everything that you allow to cross my path, for it gives me direction, strength, and wisdom, Amen.

Verse 152

"O Lord, I will honor and praise your name, for you are my God. You do such wonderful things! You planned them long ago, and now you have accomplished them." (Isaiah 25:1)

Words for thought:

Let us always keep our gaze fixed on the Lord. When our eyes are focused on Him, we continually move in the right direction. Don't be drawn away by the enemy and all His lies, because his role is to disrupt and darken our lives. His role is to always remind us where we came from; that sick, Dr. Jekyll and Mr. Hyde sort of person who couldn't be trusted or relied upon. It is up to us to strengthen our faith in God's Word and remain spiritually fit, one day at a time, so the next time Satan tries to distract us with a drink, we are strong in God's promises.

Let us pray:
Dear Heavenly Father, thank you for all your comfort and strength, Amen.

Verse 153

"The Lord says, 'I will guide you along the best pathway for your life. I will advise you and watch over you.'" (Psalm 32:8)

***Words for thought*:**

God saved us from ourselves and He will show us the path of life. He took our mess and turned it into a message so we may help the next person who reaches out their hand. God's Word encourages us to meditate on His message and to listen quietly for Him, because He will speak through our heart, and instruct and teach us in the way we should go. The Lord is calling us to have a deep relationship with Him. He wants us to admit our alcoholism, accept it, and surrender it all to Him. He wants to lift our obsession to drink and remove our character defects so we can live the life He has called us to lead. If we allow the peace of God to rule our hearts and we stay steadfast in our sobriety, God will make life beyond our wildest dreams!

Let us pray:
Dear Heavenly Father, thank you for walking with me through every season of my life, Amen.

Verse 154

"I can do all this through Him who gives me strength."
(Philippians 4:13)

Words for thought:

We cannot make progress if we do not allow God to release us from our past. For as long as we hold onto our drink problem and all the calamity it brings, we will know no peace. But if we so choose this new way of life in the hands of God as our guide, then our future has such promise. But we must not let the enemy, the enemy of fear, stand in our way. There are many things that will threaten our sobriety in this world, but our trust, faith, and love for God will see us through.

Let us pray:
Dear Heavenly Father, thank you for taking away my heavy burdens, Amen.

Verse 155

"So get rid of all the filth and evil in your lives, and humbly accept the word God has planted in your hearts, for it has the power to save your souls." (James 1:21)

Words for thought:

We use to waken with the desperation of a drink. It wasn't a matter of how or what, but always the question was when—when can I take that first drink. The minute our eyes opened in the morning, we sought a strategy of how we can drink today without getting drunk. But we now know the answer to this riddle, because it is impossible for us alcoholics to safely have just one, so we can be rest assured it is always the first drink that gets us drunk. We nearly had ourselves committed to an alcoholic death when we were shown a way out. We were shown by the grace of God that we never have to put another drink to our lips again, if we followed Him. We learn through one another that every word of God proves true, and that He is a shield to all who come to Him for protection (Proverbs 30:5). So when we wake in the morning, ask God, "Please help me stay away from a drink today."

Let us pray:
Dear Heavenly Father, thank you for giving me a choice of how I will spend my day today, Amen.

Verse 156

"Commit your actions to the Lord, and your plans will succeed." (Proverbs 16:3)

Words for thought:

When we struggle, we need to stop and ask God if we are in agreement with what He wants for us, because once we become sober, we all witness Him bring order out of chaos, good from evil, and peace out of turmoil. Even though we may sometimes fall back on our own self will, fleshly desires, and pleasures, God still wants to be in relationship with us. It is in this time of struggle that we remain vigilant in our prayers and continue to confess our sins to God so He can remove from us our transgressions and cleanse us from all unrighteousness.

Let us pray:
Dear Heavenly Father, thank you for being such a powerful force in my life today, Amen.

Verse 157

"Walk with the wise and become wise; associate with
fools and get in trouble." (Proverbs 13:20)

Words for thought:

Most of us lived in denial for a long time with our alcohol addiction. We had ourselves convinced we had everything under control. As long as we were functioning, it shouldn't matter that we rewarded ourselves by getting drunk. But that is not all we did, because our drunkenness was destroying our relationships with families and friends. It kept us from important events in our children's lives, and it kept us from being honest, loyal, and faithful to our spouses. We lived in denial of the pain and agony our families struggled with while watching us deteriorate day after day, week after week, and year after year. It never occurred to us that we couldn't stop drinking until we failed each and every day not to drink. Yet, one day we heard a voice, a small voice inside our head telling us there was a solution to our problem, and we were led by the hand of God to recovery. We learned through the twelve-step program of how to "put the plug in the jug" and become one with God. We learned His Word is full of truth and it is constant, never changing. God made our body as the temple of the Holy Spirit, and this Spirit lives in us and was given to us by God. We do not belong to ourselves, because God bought us with a price, and we must honor God with our body (1 Corinthians 6:19-20). Remember, God's Word is supreme and if we follow it we will live in His glory, truth, and never-ending love.

Let us pray:

Dear Heavenly Father, thank you for the strength and encouragement you give me through your word, Amen.

Verse 158

"Such love has no fear, because perfect love expels all fear. If we are afraid, it is for fear of punishment, and this shows that we have not fully experienced His perfect love." (1 John 4:18)

Words for thought:

God and fear do not go together, and we have come to learn that fear is one of Satan's favorite tools to bring us back to the bottom of the bottle. It keeps us from having soundness of mind. God wants to restore us to sanity. He wants to replace our fearful thoughts with His Word. Scripture tells us to live as God's obedient children. It says do not slip back into our old ways of living to satisfy our own desires, because we didn't know better. Now we must be holy in everything we do, just as God who chose us is holy (1 Peter 1:14-15).

Let us pray:
Dear Heavenly Father, thank you for the immeasurable amount of love you have for me, Amen.

Verse 159

God saved you by His grace when you believed and you can't take credit for this; it is a gift from God. Salvation is not a reward for the good things we have done, so none of us can boast about it. For we are God's masterpiece. He has created us anew in Christ Jesus, so we can do the good things He planned for us long ago. (Ephesians 2:8-10)

Words for thought:

God must take priority in our life above all else. We do not resist when He convicts us, because sometimes we stray away from His chosen path. If we persist in our old ways, He will hold privileges and blessings from us until we again align His will with our own. All of God's works are behind the scenes, and we must have faith that in His time, it will be perfect. When we stay away from a drink one day at a time and we do not resist correction from God and we get all the advice and instruction we can, we will be wise the rest of our lives. Remember: we can make many plans, but the Lord's purpose will prevail (Proverbs 19:20-21).

Let us pray:
Dear Heavenly Father, thank you for all the things you do, that I never see, Amen.

Verse 160

"Uphold me according to your promise, that I may live; and let me not be put to shame in my hope! Hold me up, that I may be safe and have regard for your statutes continually." (Psalm 119:116-117)

Words for thought:

John Barleycorn wished upon us low self-esteem, a poor self-image, and a lack of confidence. This way of living became torturous and it magnified our drinking problem. Putting a drink to our lips was like making a deal with Satan; we knew we shouldn't, but alcohol had us selling our soul to him every single day. However, in the meantime God called us to Him, saying, "Do not be afraid or discouraged, for I the Lord will personally go ahead you. I will be with you; I will neither fail you nor abandon you" (Deuteronomy 31:8). So today we put all our trust and faith in God, and if we remain sober, we can just watch the amazing things that happen. God is our protector; let us put all our confidence in Him, and watch the many blessings unfold.

Let us pray:
Dear Heavenly Father, thank you God for changing me from the inside out, Amen.

Verse 161

"And my God will liberally supply your every need according to His riches in glory in Christ Jesus." (Philippians 4:19)

Words for thought:

God did not design us to live life alone, but that is exactly where He found us: isolated, alone, frightened, angry, depressed, dispirited, and drunk. We were so blinded by ego, pride, and self-justification. Yet, at our deepest core, we did not want to be drunk. We did not want to disappoint family and friends. We did not want to live the life of a drunk anymore, but we just could not live life sober. It wasn't until we were touched by the hand of God and became open, honest, and willing that we could take a look at our disease. An illness that steals everything, including one's life. Yet, God offered us salvation, and in return all we have to do is believe that He alone can rescue us, because He is our refuge, our place of safety; He is our God and we are to trust Him. He will rescue us from every trap and He will protect us from our disease. God's faithful promises are our armor and protection (Psalm 91:1-4).

Let us pray:

Dear Heavenly Father, thank you for the bountiful of blessings you have bestowed upon me, Amen.

Verse 162

"For the Lord your God is living among you. He is a mighty Savior. He will take delight in you with gladness. With His love, He will calm all your fears. He will rejoice over you with joyful songs." (Zephaniah 3:17)

Words for thought:

We, who are alcoholics, must learn to reeducate our mind. Our program gives us a toolbox so we may think differently about our alcoholism. It teaches us that as long as we do not pick up that first drink, then we cannot get drunk. It also teaches us about God, and we come to know He causes everything to work together for the good of those who love Him and are called according to His purpose for them (Romans 8:28). God is always with us, but the question is, are we always with God? God's grace is generous and He has given each of us a gift from His great variety of spiritual gifts. Let us use them well to serve one another (1 Peter 4:10).

Let us pray:
Dear Heavenly Father, thank you for your protection over my life, Amen.

Verse 163

"The human mind is the most deceitful of all things. No one can understand how deceitful it is." (Jeremiah 17:9)

Words for thought:

When we enter our program, we learn to accept we no longer live for ourselves. We make the choice to focus on others as well. God has set us free, warning we do not use this freedom to satisfy our own flesh, but to serve others humbly in love (Galatians 5:13). We must choose to discipline our hearts to God's word so we may experience His comfort, stability, and grace. We once felt undeserving of God's love, but after learning of His guidance we discovered His great love for us is all we need. Fellowshipping teaches us willingness, honesty, and open-mindedness, which brings us to a place God intended us to be, for this we can be grateful.

Let us pray:
Dear Heavenly Father, thank you that I can trust your word for my everyday living, Amen.

Verse 164

"Blessed is the man that endureth temptation: for when he is tried, he shall receive the crown of life, which the Lord hath promised to them that love Him." (James 1:12)

Words for thought:

Temptation will always be a battle because alcohol is every-where, and Satan thrives on our restless, irritable, discontented, drunk selves. He gives us what feels good now: instant gratification. However, God gives us what will last till eternity if we obey His Word. We will face adversity from time to time, however, what doesn't kill us makes us stronger, and if we persevere and never give up, our work will be rewarded (2 Chronicles 15:7). So in sober mind, let us move forward with good cheer, knowing God's got this!

Let us pray:

Dear Heavenly Father, thank you for keeping me protected from the hands of Satan, Amen.

Verse 165

"Imitate God, therefore, in everything you do, because you are His dear children." (Ephesians 5:1)

Words for thought:

What has us not honoring God today? Is it drunkenness, selfishness, jealousy, bitterness, resentments, hostility, self-seeking motives and/or fear? If we are living by these thoughts, we will find ourselves falling back into old patterns, old habits and old ways of thinking. If we choose, we can honor God by living in His fruits: love, joy, peace, patience, kindness, goodness, gentleness, faithfulness, and self-control (Galatians 5:22-23). The Word tells us that "God has called us to live Holy lives, not impure lives. Therefore, anyone who refuses to live by these rules is not obeying human teaching but is rejecting God, who gives His Holy Spirit to you" (1 Thessalonians 4:7-8).

Let us pray:
Dear Heavenly Father, thank you for giving me free will to choose the life I will live today. May it always be aligned with your gracious will, Amen.

Verse 166

"Let us then approach God's throne of grace with confidence, so that we may receive mercy and find grace to help us in our time of need." (Hebrews 4:16)

Words for thought:

G race: the free given, unmerited favor and love of God. This is what we receive when we choose to live a sober life every day. We pray to God for Him to make us understand how wonderful this gift is. This virtue can only come from our Father. We are made to live in perfect peace with our Lord, so let us trust in Him and keep our eyes fixed on Him, for the Lord is our eternal rock (Isaiah 26:3-4).

Let us pray:
Dear Heavenly Father, thank you for giving me grace and mercy to live my life, Amen.

Verse 167

"Jesus looked at them and said, with man this is impossible, but with God all things are possible." (Matthew 19:26)

Words for thought:

Everything was out of order in our lives, and the booze took top priority. Every day, we planned our lives around the alcohol. Everything was wrong; nothing seemed right. Neither our past, present, nor future were important; only the next drink. The day we declared we were alcoholics was the *first* day of the rest of our lives because God heard our plea. He came rushing to our aid to hold us on higher ground until we could safely move forward in sobriety. God has great things planned for our lives, but we cannot quit before the miracle happens! We are to trust in the Lord and do good, and when we take delight in Him, He will give us the desires of our heart. And when we commit our way to the Lord and trust in Him, He will make our righteous reward shine like the dawn, and He will make our vindication like the noonday sun (Psalm 37:3-6).

Let us pray:
Dear Heavenly Father, thank you for bringing order in my life from all its chaos, Amen.

Verse 168

"Wine is a mocker, a strong drink riots brawler; and whoever errs or reels because of it is not wise." (Proverbs 20:1)

Words for thought:

A lcohol over time became our worst nightmare. It slowly took away our health, dignity, and sanity. It brought us to a place of pure insanity. However, we have learned through fellowship that we have a choice: the will of God or our addiction. When we admit, accept, and surrender to the disease of alcoholism, God, over time, brings us back to soundness of mind, stability, and good judgment. His Word provides, delivers, and promises He gives His strength to the weary and increases the power of the weak (Isaiah 40:29).

Let us pray:
Dear Heavenly Father, thank you for rescuing me when I didn't know I needed it, Amen.

Verse 169

*"And we are instructed to turn from godless living
and sinful pleasures. We should live in this evil world
with wisdom, righteousness, and devotion to God."
(Titus 2:12)*

Words for thought:

Did you know we must first die to self so that God can live
in us? We cannot live on our way of doing things. Any per-
ceived idea we have for ourselves has to be smashed in order
for God to do His will in us. It takes courage for us to let go
and let God. When He is our focal point, we leave no room for
evil, and we must leave our anger behind, for if not, it will give
foothold to the devil (Ephesians 4:27). We will find peace in
God's Word when we turn away from evil and do good. We will
honor and extol His greatness, lovingkindness, and truth with
praise and worship with all the days on Earth.

Let us pray:
*Dear Heavenly Father, thank you that when my heart strays,
you quickly pull me back to your Word, Amen.*

Verse 170

"The Lord rescues the godly; He is their fortress in times of trouble. The Lord helps them, rescuing them from the wicked. He saves them, and they find shelter in Him." (Psalm 37:39-40)

Words for thought:

We, who are of the alcoholic type, have come to learn we have an allergy to alcohol. Once ingested, the rollercoaster of being drunk begins. Therefore, we must not take the first drink that gets us drunk. So what is it that will save us from these gates of an alcoholic hell? It is a complete surrender and reliance on God above. In our morning prayer, we will pray, "Listen to my voice in the morning, Lord. Each morning I bring my requests to you and wait expectantly" (Psalm 5:3).

Let us pray:
Dear Heavenly Father, thank you for hearing me when I cry out your name, Amen.

Verse 171

"God saved us and called us to be Holy, not because of what we had done, but because of His own plan and kindness. Before the world began, God planned that Christ Jesus would show us God's kindness." (2 Timothy 1:9)

Words for thought:

During our active alcoholism, we forgot everything important to us: our lives, families, jobs, finances, home, and God. Yet, in the midst of all this adversity, God hadn't forgotten about us. Although we were on the brink of breaking, God's love remained unfailing. He paved a way for us to find laughter, love, gratitude, and forgiveness. He wants us to know where two or three together as His followers He will be there among us (Matthew 18:20). And He will hold us by our right hand, because He is Lord our God and He says, "Don't be afraid, I am here with you" (Isaiah 41:13). Prayer and meditation on Scripture will strengthen our faith on all things above.

Let us pray:
Dear Heavenly Father, thank you for opening my mind and heart to your Word, Amen.

Verse 172

"Pride ends in humiliation, while humility brings honor." (Proverbs 29:23)

Words for thought:

All of us go into drinking thinking that it is all fun and glamorous. Most of us were not even close to the legal drinking age before we had our first glass of alcohol. Instantly we felt that warm and fuzzy feeling. We couldn't quite explain it, but we felt as if we had arrived. We began to think early on that the booze was the solution to all our problems, but years and years later, we discovered we drank because we liked the effect and damn to all its consequences. Yet, those of us who woke up one day and said, "I cannot live this way anymore," had our first spiritual awakening. God offered us a chance at self-realization, a chance to realize our ego, pride, self-importance, and fear. We stepped into the realm of recovery and learned one day at a time not to drink. God allowed a shift in our consciousness for us to see and feel the damage and destruction we caused along our life's path. He enlightened our heart so we could make amends for all the upset and turmoil we caused family and friends. Remember, God is our strong fortress, and He makes our way perfect (2 Samuel 22:33).

Let us pray:
Dear Heavenly Father, thank you for giving me another solution to my disease, Amen.

Verse 173

"And you must love the Lord your God with all your heart, all your soul, all your mind, and all your strength. The second is equally important: love your neighbor as yourself. No other commandment is greater than these." (Mark 12:30-31)

Words for thought:

So we started drinking at a young age and it was fun having late night dates and parties. We were living the dream, until we weren't. We discovered friends slipped away, family pulled away in despair, and our life passed us by, with us wondering, "How did I get this drunk again?" Miraculously, we found a solution to our drinking problem and He is amazing! God knew of our agony, transgressions, and misdeeds in advance, but He loved us anyway. His Word tells us "this is real love--not that we loved God, but that He loved us and sent His Son as a sacrifice to take away our sins" (1 John 4:10). So we now know as an alcoholic that there is light at the end of the tunnel, but there is work to be done. So the question is, are we willing to go to any length to get sober? Are we willing to put our program of recovery first as a priority? Are we honest enough to confess our sins daily to our Lord? Are we open enough to share with others what we received so freely? God gave us life to live sober and not as a drunkard. He wants us to be filled with gratitude and love, not only for each other, but for ourselves, while remembering, "We love each other because He loved us first" (1 John 4:19).

Let us pray:

Dear Heavenly Father, thank you for showering me with the love I didn't think I deserved, Amen.

Verse 174

"My heart may fail, and my spirit may grow weak, but God remains the strength of my heart; He is mine forever." (Psalm 73:26)

Words for thought:

We all show weaknesses in certain areas of our life. The "normal temperate" drinker shows less glaring shortcomings than our own, but we all share them. When we rely upon God, He will turn those defects into our greatest strengths. See, God did not create us to focus on everything we are not, but to seek everything that He is: loving, kind, forgiving, patient, unshakable, and powerful. We need to remember "the earth is the Lord's, and everything in it. The world and all its people belong to Him" (Psalm 24:1). So when we struggle or feel weak or when we feel despair, let us have faith that the Spirit will help us in our weaknesses. If we do not know how to pray, the Holy Spirit will pray for us with groaning that cannot be expressed in words (Romans 8:26). Hallelujah!

Let us pray:
Dear Heavenly Father, thank you that Your word is unwavering, Amen.

Verse 175

*"Now to him who is able to do immeasurably more
than all we ask or imagine, according to His power
that is at work within us." (Ephesians 3:20)*

Words for thought:

It is by God's grace that we are sober today, but it is by our
choice if we continue our journey seeking emotional sobriety.
The pathway of God will lead us to His guidance, purpose, and
power. His Word promises us that He can do more than we can
ask or imagine, because nothing is impossible for Him. We are
not promised to be free of any intense feelings of our disease or
free from life problems related to our alcoholism, however, He
will provide a safe avenue for us to grow from our experiences
instead of drinking over them. God wants us to have all the
power to understand, as all His people should, how wide, long,
high, and deep His love is for us. He wants us to experience the
love of Christ, even though it is too great to understand fully,
because then we will be made complete with all the fullness of
life and power that comes from Him (Ephesians 3:18-19).

Let us pray:
*Dear Heavenly Father, thank you that I may come to you in
prayer anywhere, anytime of my day, Amen.*

Verse 176

"In your anger do not sin. Do not let the sun go down while you are still angry and do not give the devil a foothold." (Ephesians 4:26-27)

Words for thought:

A nger is a great motivator for our alcoholism and so is bitterness, guilt, shame, resentment, envy, jealousy, and isolation. God did not create us to live alone, apart from one another, with such hatred in our hearts. See, these defects of character will only allow us to continue walking in the darkness opposed to the light and God tells us to "look after each other so that none of us fails to receive His grace" and we are to watch out so "no poisonous root of bitterness grows up to trouble us, corrupting many" (Hebrews 12:15). God calls us to fulfill His purpose, saying, "You didn't choose me. I chose you. I appointed you to go and produce lasting fruit, so that the Father will give you whatever you ask for, using my name" (John 15:16). So, let us take all our fears, discomfort, anxieties, and worries and bring them before God so He can forgive us our trespasses and cleanse them all away.

Let us pray:
Dear Heavenly Father, thank you for your guidance that renews for me each morning, Amen.

Verse 177

"'Get out of here, Satan,' Jesus told him. For the Scriptures say, 'You must worship the Lord your God and serve Him only.'" (Matthew 4:10)

Words for thought:

Our enemy is attacking us every day. He is waiting patiently for the day that a crack appears in our foundation. He idly waits for our disease to begin taunting us "just one won't hurt," and unless we are spiritually fit in the word of God, it won't take long for Satan to tear our house down. We must wash ourselves in God's Word as a part of our morning prayer time so Satan cannot get a foothold on us. We must align our hearts with God's will for our lives and discipline our walk of faith in Him so when our obsession to drink begins we have the mental defenses to ward off the first drink. And by putting on all God's armor, we will be able to stand firm against all strategies of the devil saying, "No, not today Satan!"

Let us pray:
Dear Heavenly Father, thank you for the ability to seek your Word one day at a time, Amen.

Verse 178

"Remember, it is sin to know what you ought to do and then not do it." (James 4:17)

Words for thought:

Our minds are filled with so many different emotions throughout the day, and we are so much more than our feelings. Instead of thinking about drinking upon awakening, we can focus our attention on seeking God's plan for us instead. God will meet us right where we are, as long as we come to Him with a humble heart. When negative thinking seeps in, we will reject it with God's Word, so it does not begin to steal our joy. We have the option today to live in God's Word with mercy, grace, guidance and truth, so in prayer today, let us ask God for the privilege to enhance our growing, meaningful relationship with Him.

Let us pray:
Dear Heavenly Father, thank you for leading me to your truth, your word, Amen.

Verse 179

*"And lead us not into temptation, but deliver us from
evil: for thine is the kingdom, and the glory, forever."
(Matthew 6:13)*

Words for thought:

Our fellowship and our sobriety helps us to stop pretending to
be everything that we are not. We were addicts filled with
rage, delusion, laziness, pride, dishonesty, fear, pain, and suffering, but that is all over now. It is over because we finally
chose God over the bottle. One day we found God and made
a decision to yield our will to Him. We followed a few simple
rules from our recovery program and allowed God, and those
He put in our lives to love us until we could love ourselves. God
gave us time to heal and to gain wisdom into our illness and He
tells us in the Bible that "to acquire wisdom is to love yourself;
people who cherish understanding will prosper" (Proverbs 19:8).

Let us pray:
*Dear Heavenly Father, thank you for saving me from my own
disgrace, Amen.*

Verse 180

"Trust in the Lord with all your heart; and lean not unto thine own understanding. In all ways acknowledge Him, and He shall direct thy paths." (Proverbs 3:5-6)

Words for thought:

As Scripture tells us we are not to lean on our own understanding. In fact, a part of our recovery is to "humbly ask God to remove our shortcomings." He will take our failures and weaknesses, our faults and our sins; He will take our disease, our sickness and our failed inebriated past and give us a clean slate every single twenty-four hours. We can have faith that all of God's fruits and promises will be fulfilled when we follow His indescribable pathway for our lives.

Let us pray:
Dear Heavenly Father, thank you for the many gifts that you have bestowed on my life in sobriety, Amen.

Verse 181

"He existed before anything else, and He holds all creation together." (Colossians 1:17)

Words for thought:

God already knows all about our illness, flaws, and weaknesses. However, let us not allow these things to keep us from His wonderful glory. When we find ourselves not following Him wholeheartedly, we mustn't become discouraged, because His forgiveness is abundant. He will never be shocked if or when we fail Him because even His Word tells us that everyone has sinned and that we have all fallen short of His glorious standard (Romans 3:23). However, His restoration is quickly available when we fall short of His perfect love.

Let us pray:
Dear Heavenly Father, thank you that all I have to do is come to you and whisper your name and you hear me, Amen.

Verse 182

"Trust in the Lord with all your heart; do not depend on your own understanding." (Proverbs 3:5)

Words for thought:

The only avenue in understanding God's way is to study His Word. We need to listen carefully when He teaches us through people, places, and things. He will give us lessons on keeping sober, and teaches on things like forgiveness, love, trust, and acceptance. God will lead us to where He wants us to go, so let us meditate in His presence. He will protect us when we turn to Him in prayer. He has given us new life to live; abundantly, joyfully, and bountifully to its fullest!

Let us pray:
Dear Heavenly Father, thank you for supplying me with the Bible that is full of your wisdom, Amen.

Verse 183

"We know that God doesn't listen to sinners, but He is ready to hear those who worship Him and do His will." (John 9:31)

Words for thought:

When we cry out to God with all of our hearts, He reveals Himself to us. We pray, "Help us, O God of our salvation! Help us for the glory of your name. Save us and forgive our sins for the honor of your name" (Psalm 79:9). Fill our mind, will, and emotions with your wisdom and bring clarity to our lives. Lift this obsession of alcohol that has us in its grips and near death. God, shower us with your perfect will so our lives will overflow with your grace. Thank you, Lord, for hearing our prayer. Hallelujah!

Let us pray:
Dear Heavenly Father, thank you for being my sovereign God in all things, Amen.

Verse 184

*"Sin is no longer your master, for you no longer live
under the requirements of the law, you live under the
freedom of God's grace." (Romans 6:14)*

Words for thought:

We came to God with our sin and shame and laid them at
the alter, because He said "come to me, all of you who
are weary and carry heavy burdens, and I will give you rest"
(Matthew 11:28). He gra-ciously set free from our mind, will,
and emotions the guilt, shame, and remorse we carried day after
da. The humiliation that kept us in the bottle is gone. Only God
can give us freedom to live on this earth with mercy and grace.
Let us come to Him boldly and shout Hallelujah!

Let us pray:
*Dear Heavenly Father, thank you for removing the agony that
once filled my heart, Amen.*

Verse 185

"Let my tongue sing about your word, for all your commands are right." (Psalm 119:172)

Words for thought:

We, "the addicted type", cannot face our shortcomings of bitterness, resentments, or envy without drinking. Yet, what we can live with sober are the fruits that God gives us instead: love, joy, peace, patience, kindness, goodness, gentleness, faithfulness, and self-control. These fruits of the spirit given to us in Galatians 5 are given by the grace of God to replace anything hurting in our hearts. Let us not be the obnoxious, fall down, slurring drunk at the party anymore, but instead be the peacemaker in the midst of trouble, because God so loves those who control their tongue. Scripture even says, "If you want to enjoy life and see many happy days, keep your tongue from speaking evil and your lips from telling lies" (1 Peter 3:10).

Let us pray:
Dear Heavenly Father, thank you for giving me your Scripture so I may see people, places, and things in a different light, Amen.

Verse 186

"Understand, therefore, that the Lord your God is indeed God. He is the faithful God who keeps His covenant for a thousand generations and lavishes His unfailing love on those who love Him and obey His commands." (Deuteronomy 7:9)

Words for thought:

Do we believe we were all created in God's image? Well, we should, because it says, "God created human beings in His own image. In the image of God He created them; male and female He created them" (Genesis 1:27). How about this: do we believe love all started with God's love for us? Simply put, yes, because Scripture tells us in 1 John 4:19, "We love each other because He loved us first." See, this is the reason why we can love one another: because He first loved us! Do we have enough love for ourselves to abstain from alcohol, one day at a time? If we so choose, we may believe God showed us the greatest love of all when He allowed His only Son Jesus Christ to die on the cross for us. So God has prepared to bring us to a place of safety and serenity, but are we willingly, openly, and honestly ready to accept this gift?

Let us pray:
Dear Heavenly Father, thank you for helping me by giving me a choice, Amen.

Verse 187

"Whatever you have learned or received or heard from me, or seen in me, put into practice and the God of peace will be with you." (Philippians 4:9)

Words for thought:

When we align our mind, will, and emotions with God's will for our day, then it begins to make sense. We do not have to try to be someone that we are not by pouring alcohol down our throats any time of the day. Alcohol made us withdrawn and unlovable. It flooded our hearts with isolation, anger, fear, temptation, and torment. We were self-destructing until we discovered God and fellowshipping. We stopped sabotaging ourselves and began to accept some of God's many gifts. Gifts of salvation, forgiveness, grace, dignity, assurance, and hope. Slowly, we are embracing who we are in Christ, without the booze. Remember, we only have a daily reprieve for our alcoholism. Every day is a brand-new start to our life! Hallelujah, God's faithful love never ends and His mercies never cease (Lamentations 3:22).

Let us pray:
Dear Heavenly Father, thank you for seeing me in ways that I cannot see myself, Amen.

Verse 188

"Because of Christ and our faith in Him, we can now come boldly and confidently into God's presence."
(Ephesians 3:12)

Words for thought:

When we enter the program and begin to receive the many gifts of sobriety, we begin to realize our craving for a drink has lessened. We no longer have the need to choose the road of selfishness and self-seeking ways. We then surrender and begin to accept God's Holy Spirit on our lives. We slowly begin to accept His guidance, love, and forgiveness. God will make all things new for those of us who earnestly seek Him and He promises to wait patiently for us to surrender our disease to His holy name, so then He can lift us up out of our pit of despair.

Let us pray:
Dear Heavenly Father, thank you for allowing me to come to you freely and boldly, Amen.

Verse 189

*"Lord, hear my prayer, listen to my cry for mercy;
in your faithfulness and righteousness come to my
relief." (Psalm 143:1)*

Words for thought:

A t some point, our whole lives began falling apart. It became
so easy to focus on the pain, problems, and sinful thoughts.
We felt God didn't love us anymore because we were so damaged. Our minds were filled with so much angst and we lived
in this world of fear, pain, and suffering. However, through all
this affliction, the one thing that remained new every morning
is God's faithfulness to us, His compassion for us, His love
that never fails us. It is important to wait on God for all things,
because He will lead us by His truth and He will teach us, for
He is the God who saves us; all day we can put our hope in
Him (Psalm 25:5).

Let us pray:
*Dear Heaven Father, thank you for hearing my cry in the midst
of my woes, Amen.*

Verse 190

"He forgives all my sins and heals all my diseases. He redeems me from death and crowns me with love and tender mercies." (Psalm 103:3-5)

Words for thought:

W hen we entered into the rooms of recovery, we come in broken, beaten, and shattered. We did not know how to put the drink down. Then we heard of a higher power, God, and we begin to accept His powerful message. We surrender and He transforms us and molds us in sobriety. He changes our whole attitude on life and in return we praise Him with our whole heart. And we praise Him so we never forget the good things He does for us (Psalm 103:1-2).

Let us pray:
Dear Heavenly Father, thank you for shaping me into the person I've become, Amen.

Verse 191

*"So let's not get tired of doing what is good. At just
the right time we will reap a harvest of blessing if we
don't give up." (Galatians 6:9)*

Words for thought:

In the end, we lived in fear, doubt, and anxiety. We knew of
God, but we were not sure if His love for us could bring us
out of this insanity. We were lost in this getting up, drink, drink
some more, get sloshed, pass out, and then start all over again
the next day, while expecting different results. The day God
spoke to each and every one of us, and He did, was the day of
our miracle. We learned the only approval we needed is that
which mattered to God. He led us to a complete change of mind,
will, and emotions. Now after receiving our saving grace, we
need to walk with our Lord every day and we must reflect His
behavior in all we do and say, because we have to show the next
suffering alcoholic that we are restored, because God called
us by name.

Let us pray:
Dear Heavenly Father, thank you for showing me the good harvest in my life, Amen.

Verse 192

"For everything comes from Him and exists by His power and is intended for His glory. All glory to Him forever." (Romans 11:36)

Words for thought:

O nce we fully concede to the belief that all things have been created through God and for God, we can rest. We are no longer the director of the show! We now know after admitting our alcoholism that we put it in God's hands and He will provide for everything we need before we even ask; simple! Remember, He pulled us from our deepest, darkest nightmare of dependency and no matter the problem, no matter the despair, emotional, physical, financial, whenever or wherever we hit rock bottom, God was there to pick us up. So, therefore we glorify His name.

Let us pray:
Dear Heavenly Father, thank you for opening my soul to your love, Amen.

Verse 193

*"His divine power has given us everything we need for
a godly life through our knowledge of Him who called
us by His own glory and goodness." (2 Peter 1:3)*

Words for thought:

We have been given the free and unmerited favor of God when
we cried His name in our beaten-down hell called addiction. He saved us after hearing our sobbing. He felt our pain,
so He offered us healing through His Word. His Word gives
us many resources for our journey of sobriety. It is through
the fellowship and God's Word that we receive this generous
gift of forgiveness and God's Word says, "Make allowance
for each other's faults, and forgive anyone who offends you.
Remember, the Lord forgave you, so you must forgive others"
(Colossians 3:13).

Let us pray:
*Dear Heavenly Father, thank you for the glorious gift of for-
giveness, Amen.*

Verse 194

"So, dear brothers and sisters work hard to prove that you really are among those God has called and chosen. Do these things, and you will never fall away." (2 Peter 1:10)

Words for thought:

I t is such a miracle that even after all the destruction we caused in our path with our alcoholism that God, by His divine power, has given us everything we need for living a sober life. Because of all His marvelous glory and excellence, He has given us great and precious promises. These promises enable us to share His divine nature so we may escape the world's corruption caused by our own human desires. We must make every effort to respond to God's promises. We are to supplement our faith with moral excellence, and moral excellence with knowledge, and knowledge with self-control, and self-control with patient endurance, and patient endurance with godliness, and godliness with brotherly affection with love for everyone, and the more we grow like this, the more productive and useful we will be in our knowledge for our Lord Jesus Christ (2 Peter 1:1-8).

Let us pray:
Dear Heavenly Father, thank you for rescuing me from myself, Amen.

Verse 195

"Teach me to do your will, for you are my God. May your gracious Spirit lead me forward on a firm footing." (Psalm 143:10)

Words for thought:

Our minds were once filled with impure thoughts, agony, laziness, mental suffering, affliction, distress, and joylessness. However, we were told if we put the drink down, our lives will become manageable, and that our flesh will not scream out in misery. If we come to believe in step two, then we will no longer fight the battle of alcoholism alone and we shall not have an altruistic attitude toward our fellowman, for we have slowly learned to let go and let God! We suddenly realize God has done for us that which we could not do by ourselves, and we slowly discover that nothing this world offers will satisfy our drink problem. God tells us "wine produces mockers; alcohol leads to brawls. Those led astray by drink cannot be wise" (Proverbs 20:1). So now that we know the difference we pray, "And don't let us yield to temptation, but rescue us from the evil one" (Matthew 6:13).

Let us pray:
Dear Heavenly Father, thank you for saving me from my own disgrace, Amen.

Verse 196

"If you want to enjoy life and see many happy days, keep your tongue from speaking evil and your lips from telling lies. Turn away from evil and do good. Search for peace and work to maintain it." (1 Peter 3:10-11)

Words for thought:

In the battlefield of our addiction, we completely lost all integrity. Our temptation to do evil outweighed any opportunity we had to be a useful person to our loved ones. Our standards, decency, sincerity, reliability, and moral character all became less important, because we only wanted the drink. Yet, during our addiction, God paved a way. A way out of our desperation. What is so amazing about God is that He delights in doing big things in our lives, one day at a time. We will not know His plan, but we will keep our hope, and we will not lose faith, for it is written, "the Lord is good to everyone. He showers compassion on all His creation" (Psalm 145:9).

Let us pray:
Dear Heavenly Father, thank you, for your guidance. It has enabled me to live life on your terms, Amen.

Verse 197

"For I can do everything through Christ, who gives me strength," (Philippians 4:13)

Words for thought:

We face a thousand decisions in our upcoming twenty-four hours ahead. To the alcoholic, whose mind is warped by the drink, decisions are not made out of good wisdom. Be that as it is, we have a choice. A program that offers us a second chance at life, sober. When we ask, God will take our eyes off our individual drink problem and reveal we are not alone, because He is near, and His ways are far beyond anything that we could imagine. He gave us healing and forgiveness, and He fought our demon with us, and now we are free to do God's will on Earth as it is in heaven. Hallelujah!

Let us pray:
Dear Heavenly Father, thank you for allowing me to align my will with yours, Amen.

Verse 198

"Run from anything that stimulates youthful lusts. Instead, pursue righteous living, faithfulness, love, and peace. Enjoy the companionship of those who call on the Lord with pure hearts." (2 Timothy 2:22)

Words for thought:

In our youth as we grew older our addictions robbed us of purpose, growth, focus, and future plans. It stole from us the time we could have spent in God's presence. Our choices were blinded over and over again by us choosing the drink, until we couldn't face another day drunk. In the throes of our weaknesses, denial, and shame, we cried out to you, and you God, carried us. We weren't even sure if this God thing worked yet, but slowly we discovered the spiritual side of things. We slowly accepted God absorbed our sins from us. He began removing character defects and He kept a clear path for us to see our wrongs. He then gave us opportunities to set things right. From this day forward, we must continue on our journey with God, stay in program, remain sober, and pass along "how it works" to the next person who walks through the doors.

Let us pray:
Dear Heavenly Father, thank you for showing me the pathway to recovery, Amen.

Verse 199

"Those who belong to Christ Jesus have nailed the passions and desires of their sinful nature to His cross and crucified them there." (Galatians 5:24)

Words for thought:

In sobriety, we've learned not to conform to the unrighteous life of our alcoholism. God made us see we lived by the standards of our flesh and not the Holy Spirit. He patiently planned our ultimate path and waited for us to follow, and eventually we did. We have a daily choice we must make: our will or God's will. If we so choose and believe the commandments of the Lord are right, then they will bring joy to our heart. Because the commands of the Lord are clear, they will give us insight for living (Psalm 19:8).

Let us pray:
Dear Heavenly Father, thank you for the shield of protection on my life, Amen.

Verse 200

*"So don't worry about tomorrow, for tomorrow will
bring its own worries. Today's trouble is enough for
today." (Matthew 6:34)*

Words for thought:

When we become sober, we learn to live life one day at a
time, with God. We turn our attention away from the things
of this world. We suddenly find ourselves no longer dissatisfied because God has offered us a fresh start, a new beginning.
"This means that anyone who belongs to Christ has become
a new person. The old life is gone; a new life has begun" (2
Corinthians 5:17). We give praise and glory to our God for
being our source of hope amidst all the chaos, and we praise
Him because we no longer walk this earth alone, afraid, lost,
and drunk.

Let us pray:
*Dear Heavenly Father, thank you for giving me the gift of
eternal life, Amen.*

Verse 201

"Keep me safe, O God, for I have come to you for refuge." (Psalm 16:1)

Words for thought:

We are on our knees. We are drunk and cannot remember how or even why. Our emotions are filled with torment—the kind of torment that determines whether you want to live or die. So we cry out, "God, I need you now," and then we feel Him. We get the sense we are no longer abandoned and we are no longer alone. So we cling to God and we begin to seek His ways, His words, and His truth. Always remembering that when we come close to God, God will come close to us (James 4:8).

Let us pray:
Dear Heavenly Father, thank you for your love, your compassion, and your promises, Amen.

Verse 202

"O Lord my God, I cried to you for help, and you restored my health." (Psalm 30:2)

Words for thought:

Through our brokenness, God brought us healing. He called upon us to work on ourselves and not be the fixer of everybody else. This is the only time when we get to be selfish, because we need to get well to serve others. See we are not horrible people, but we do have a horrific disease, and alcoholic behavior makes us unpleasant, and our allergy to alcohol keeps us sick. Yet, when we surrender all this to God, He begins performing life-changing deeds in our life. We see His Word gives us great encouragement, so we must stay close to Him in prayer with a grateful heart. Remembering we are powerless on Earth, so we pray, "Thy kingdom come thy will be done in earth as it is in heaven" (Matthew 6:10).

Let us pray:
Dear Heavenly Father, thank you for recreating me with your power, Amen.

Verse 203

"Humble yourselves before the Lord, and He will lift you up." (James 4:10)

Words for thought:

God equips us with everything we need to be successful in our journey of recovery. He knows everything we need before we even ask, but His request is for us to let go of pride and humble ourselves before Him. He tells us not to be selfish and we must not try to impress others. He says to be humble, thinking of others as better than yourselves (Philippians 2:2). God will supply us with His love and direction, after all He is our rock, our fortress and our Savior in whom we find protection. He is our shield, the power that saved us, He is our place of safety (Psalm 18:2). Hallelujah!

Let us pray:

Dear Heavenly Father, thank you for being my everything, Amen.

Verse 204

"Lead me by your truth and teach me, for you are the God who saves me. All day long I put my hope in you." (Psalm 25:5)

Words for thought:

We stand before God and just pour out our brokenness to Him. Our minds that were once full of alcoholic agony, doubt, guilt, and loss of hope, can now be filled with God's Word. With God's love our hearts can begin to mend its resentments. We can get excited because God will toss any hurdle there is in front of us, as long as we believe. Look, He wants a relationship with us, but He cannot do this without our coming to Him in petition and prayer for everything. Humility, love, and gratitude will keep us filled with joy and gladness in the next twenty-four hours ahead as we shout how great is our God.

Let us pray:
Dear Heavenly Father, thank you for moving the heavens and earth just to save my soul, Amen.

Verse 205

"If another believer is overcome by some sin, you who are godly should gently and humbly help that person back onto the right path. And be careful not to fall into the same temptation yourself." (Galatians 6:1)

Words for thought:

Our battle with our alcoholism can only be sustained with a daily reprieve and we must always stay alert, because Satan does not stop nipping at our heels just because we put the drink down. Oh no, it is always when we are living the happy, joyous, and free life that He attacks. So what do we do when faced with the greatest temptation of our lives: dependency on alcohol? We turn to our only truth: God. Then we continue to maintain our spirituality and share it with others. Remember, life will not be without its tribulations and temptations, and it may not always be smooth sailing, but rest assured God knows the way out. He tells us to bring *all* our burdens to Him in faith and lay them down at His feet, for He is our refuge, and He will forever sustain us.

Let us pray:
Dear Heavenly Father, thank you that I no longer live in condemnation, Amen.

Verse 206

"But the Lord watches over those who fear Him, those who rely on His unfailing love." (Psalm 33:18)

Words for thought:

God's love is eternal. He has an everlasting love for us, His children. We must not get caught up in the busyness of this world without keeping God as our top priority. We purposely have to set time aside throughout our day to have quiet communion with Him. If we should doubt His love, we ask Him to help us with our absence of faith. Step eleven tells us, "sought through prayer and meditation to improve our conscious contact with God as we understood Him, praying only for knowledge of His will for us and the power to carry that out." God is our tool to life, the key that was always missing.

Let us pray:
Dear Heavenly Father, thank you for loving me when I could not love myself, Amen.

Verse 207

*"Once you were dead because of your disobedience
and your many sins. You use to live in sin, just like the
rest of the world, obeying the devil-the commander
of the powers in the unseen world. He is the spirit at
work in the hearts of those who refuse to obey God."
(Ephesians 2:1-2)*

Words for thought:

On any given day, we drank. We were way past deciding if we would drink in the morning because it became a necessity. If we were the functional drunk, then happy hour couldn't come soon enough, and by dinner time we were two sheets to the wind. This is how we lived day after day, month after month, and year after year. So what saved us? According to Ephesians 2:8, we were saved by God's grace when we believed, but it tells us that we are not to take credit for this saving grace because it is a gift from Him. So we move forward in prayer and meditation with hope and faith that one day at a time, we no longer need to take that first drink. Hallelujah!

Let us pray:
Dear Heavenly Father, thank you that your love endures forever, Amen.

Verse 208

"But I fear that somehow your pure and undivided devotion to Christ will be corrupted, just as Eve was deceived by the cunning ways of the serpent." (2 Corinthians 11:3)

Words for thought:

We need to sit quietly with God in prayer to refrain from any distractions of our own flesh. Satan is competing with God to earn our attention. See, the king of hell wants us to be devoted to him. He wants to devour our souls and bring us back to our delusional and meaningless lives of drunken disorder. Because of this, our zeal for God must be greater than our plight. The word of God will set us free as we pray, "Father, forgive me for my harmful ways to my physical body. I pray that my disease will not be stronger than my faith. In you Lord, I will give all the glory, all the day long!"

Let us pray:
Dear Heavenly Father, thank you that your word is alive and active in my life, Amen.

Verse 209

*"For everything there is a season, a time for every
activity under heaven. A time to be born and a time
to die. A time to plant and a time to harvest. A time to
kill and a time to heal. Time to tear down and a time
to build up. A time to cry and a time to laugh. A time
to grieve and a time to dance. A time to scatter stones
and a time to gather stones. A time to embrace and a
time to turn away. A time to search and a time to quit
searching. A time to keep and a time to throw away. A
time to tear and a time to mend. A time to be quiet and
a time to speak. A time to love and a time to hate. A
time for war and a time for peace." (Ecclesiastes 3:1-8)*

Words for thought:

We all have seasons in our life where we had everything or
we've had nothing. Change is certain, but the only entity
that will never change is God. He never abandoned us, not once
through our whole drunken existence. Even when Satan had us in
His snare, He did not leave us. Our Father waited unconditionally
for us to admit our alcoholism, and for us to fall on bended knee,
praying. Our God is an awesome God who gave His only Son to
save us. Let us sing hallelujah! It is time to bring all our sinful
ways to God so He may absorb our guilt, shame, and remorse. We
are to go forward in life sober, one day at a time, meditating on
God's Word, being sure to bring all the glory to Him!

Let us pray:
*Dear Heavenly Father, thank you for being my safe haven
throughout my years, Amen.*

Verse 210

"The Lord is close to all who call on Him, yes, to all who call on Him in truth." (Psalm 145:18)

Words for thought:

We live our lives in our addiction thinking we will never be good enough for anyone, let alone God. But, the truth is, God knew everything about us when He wove us in our mother's womb. Luke 12:7 says to us, "Even every hair on your head has been counted." God loves us and He wants to heal our hurt and pain caused by our illness, alcoholism. He wants us to gather up all our courage and take this long walk into sobriety. Remember, God always encourages us to come to Him with everything, be it sadness, anger, delight, fear, or disappointment any time of day. He wants us to hold nothing back in prayer, because He knows that our secrets will destroy us and that our truth will set us free.

Let us pray:
Dear Heavenly Father, thank you for allowing me to see my truth, Amen.

Verse 211

"But when you are praying, first forgive anyone you are holding a grudge against, so that your Father in heaven will forgive your sins too." (Mark 11:25)

Words for thought:

Unforgiveness, who does it hurt, except ourselves. If we choose to live a life of bitterness, anger, hatred, and vengefulness toward others, it will slowly bring us back to the drink. In recovery, we have steps four through seven, which are given to us so we can clean up the wreckage of our past. It is not for the person on the other end, but for our own well-being and peace of mind. Remember, God commands forgiveness as He has forgiven our sins. He is compassionate and merciful. God is slow to get angry and He is filled with unfailing love. He will not constantly accuse us for all our sins; He does not deal harshly with us, as we deserve. For His unfailing love toward those who fear Him is as great as the height of the heavens above the earth. He has removed our sins as far from us as the east is from the west (Psalm 103:8-12). We mustn't allow the wounds from our past prevent us from letting go, for our future sake, because unforgiveness will always stand before us and our God.

Let us pray:
Dear Heavenly Father, thank you for your compassion, for when I sin and repent, your forgiveness takes place, Amen.

Verse 212

"Your own ears will hear Him. Right behind you a voice will say, this is the way you should go, whether to the right or to the left." (Isaiah 30:21)

Words for thought:

In our program of recovery, we come to learn who we are in God: His children! We begin to feel His love for us and we are willing to wait for His guidance. We are no longer afraid to come boldly and confidently to Him in our prayers, because His mercy and grace showers us with all that we need. O Lord, you are a God of compassion and mercy, slow to get angry and filled with unfailing love and faithfulness (Psalm 86:15). Day by day, as our hope and faith continues to grow in His Word, we are able to become a witness to our fellow members of all the greatness that God and sobriety gives.

Let us pray:
Dear Heavenly Father, thank you for your greatness and all that you've given me, Amen.

Verse 213

"For I know that good itself does not dwell in me, that is, in my sinful nature. For I have the desire to do what is good, but I cannot carry it out." (Romans 7:18)

Words for thought:

Our own flesh lies to us. Satan baits us with our flesh, which brings only destruction, deception, and chaos. No one likes to be deceived, so let us cover ourselves in the Word of God. We will harvest great love if we obey the commandments of our Lord. Let us boast to our family and friends about everything God has done and continues to do in our lives.

Let us pray:
Dear Heavenly Father, thank you for the gift of the Holy Spirit, Amen.

Verse 214

"But when I am afraid, I will put my trust in you."
(Psalm 56:3)

Words for thought:

When God called us to Him, He offered us redemption. He called us and spared our lives from an alcoholic death because He loves us. God is willing to wipe our slate clean of our misgivings through our belief in Him. No need to stop and ask why God did this for us sinners, because we know through His Word it is because He loves us! He encourages us not to be afraid or discouraged; He will personally go ahead of us. God promises to be with us and to never fail nor abandon us (Deuteronomy 31:8). He promises to be with us in our troubles; hallelujah!

Let us pray:
Dear Heavenly Father, thank you for never abandoning me, even when I doubted you, Amen.

Verse 215

"Listen closely to my prayer, O Lord; hear my cry. I will call to you whenever I'm in trouble, and you will answer me." (Psalm 86:6-7)

Words for thought:

We spent years in isolation, feeling like an outcast, living in the misery of our own disease, feeling as though nothing could save us from that first icy glass of Grey Goose! Nevertheless, we made a decision to believe whatever we are going through, God will never abandon us, but he will give us free will! Whether we choose to believe in Him is completely up to us. But the terrific thing is we learn that we are no longer judge and jury! Oh, yes, that comfortable table we sat at with a drink in our hands judging every person, place, and thing. That grandiose and high expectation attitude we carried feeling like we're going to conquer the world, but instead, in reality, we fell face first to the ground, laughing at ourselves as a child would or we begin weeping, wondering how we again got so drunk. There is a saving grace to these last drunks, however, and it is because it's in one of these sprees that we cried out our suffering and suddenly we received God's comfort. Then, in program we received His love and in sobriety we found a new sense of freedom. Hallelujah!

Let us pray:
Dear Heavenly Father, thank you for giving me freedom from saving the world, Amen.

Verse 216

"Search me, O God, and know my heart; test me and know my anxious thoughts. Point out anything in me that offends You, and lead me along the path of everlasting life." (Psalm 139:23-24)

Words for thought:

In our active drinking days, there was so much sadness. There was plenty of pain, suffering, sickness, secrets, lies, anger, and denial. We created many hardships (the ISM'S-I sabotage myself) in our lives and we could not find our way out of the agony of our alcoholism. Then one day a solution came. It is in the form of two letters *AA* and one Big Book. Once we learned about our allergy and that we must abstain from any form of alcohol one day at a time, our mystery of insanity was explained. We discovered a power greater than ourselves, more powerful than our disease and we sing praise because oh, how does God love us! The Lord our God lives among us and He is a mighty Savior. He takes delight in us with gladness and with His love, He calms our fears. God will rejoice over us with joyful songs (Zephaniah 3:17). Hallelujah!

Let us pray:
Dear Heavenly Father, thank you for saving me from my own self destruction, Amen.

Verse 217

"Study this Book of Instruction continually. Meditate on it day and night so you will be sure to obey everything written in it. Only then will you prosper and succeed in all you do." (Joshua 1:8)

Words for thought:

God's Word will give us strength so we may grow stronger every day. When we study His Word and listen to those He sent before us who share their experience, strength and hope then our desire to drink will diminish, slowly. We are to remain spiritually fit so when life challenges our sobriety, we can turn to God instead of the drink. We are no longer going to take the lead in having things our own selfish way, but instead, we will put all our hope in God and allow His will on Earth to lead us to His everlasting and boundless love He has waiting for us. We must stay alert to God's open arms so we can be His messenger to other sick and suffering alcoholics.

Let us pray:
Dear Heavenly Father, thank you for giving me the strength to share your word, Amen

Verse 218

"I take joy in doing your will, my God, for your instructions are written on my heart." (Psalm 40:8)

Words for thought:

One day, we all come to the realization that we need to accept godly correction. The more open, honest, and willing we become, the less frightened we are. We lived in a broken world of alcoholism for a long time. Suffering was a part of daily life for us, but we thought the drink was the answer until we learned the truth. Our program offered us everything we were looking for, so what was our hesitancy? It was denial, because we thought we could possibly one day find a way to drink again safely, without repercussions. That is the story of the retired man talked about in the Big Book (p. 33). He was convinced he could drink safely once he hit retirement, but "in two months he was in a hospital, puzzled and humiliated" and further, "though a robust man at retirement, he went to pieces quickly and was dead within four years." This is the delusion of our disease it convinces us that we do not have an illness so therefore we can drink normally again one day. So the idea of ever drinking safely again must be smashed, destroyed, and obliterated from our tools at hand.

Let us pray:
Dear Heavenly Father, thank you for your instructions that bring me to soundness of mind, Amen.

Verse 219

"Remember, it is sin to know what you ought to do and then not do it." (James 4:17)

Words for thought:

So many of us wondered if recovery was possible after alcoholism. We asked if we will ever have soundness of mind. Then we find the answer to be yes! Over one hundred men and women before us say they "recovered from a seemingly hopeless state of mind and body" (BB p.xiii) and they tell us alcoholics how in the book, *Alcoholics Anonymous*. We are so fortunate that we ascertained there is a solution to our drinking problem and that we are on our way to complete recovery with a daily reprieve. So what we do now is: A) trust in God, B) don't drink, C) go to meetings, D) work the twelve steps, E) clean house, F) pass along our good news, and G) never, ever give up hope.

Let us pray:
Dear Heavenly Father, thank you for sending us, over eighty years ago, two courageous men who gave hope to all alcoholics, Amen.

Verse 220

"Give, and you will receive. Your gift will return to you in full - pressed down, shaken together to make room for more, running over, and poured into your lap. The amount you give will determine the amount you get back." (Luke 6:38)

Words for thought:

God already knew the battle of hopelessness that we were up against. He knew of the suffering we endured because of our disease. At some point, God prompted us to Avenue A, but we were too tempted by Avenue B. The road of alcohol, destruction, heartache, arguments, and brawls. For most of us, we were slaves to our alcoholism for five to ten years, while others ten to thirty years, and still more for those thirty years to recovery or death. We are the fortunate ones and it is only by God's grace that we are standing firm upon solid ground. Remember, God has given us each a gift from His great variety of spiritual gifts. We are to use them well to serve one another (1 Peter 4:10).

Let us pray:
Dear Heavenly Father, thank you for giving me the spiritual gift to serve, Amen.

Verse 221

"Then call on me when you are in trouble, and I will rescue you, and you will give me glory." (Psalm 50:15)

Words for thought:

When we are at a crossroads and we do not know what to do or say, then it is time to call on the Lord. We can cry out whatever troubles we have, because God already knows we come to Him with emotional wounds. He knows of our self-destructive ways. He knows the unthinkable we've done and the lies we told to protect our alcoholism. He knew we needed His saving long before we did. We just knew we were trapped by our own disease and knew no human aid could save us. God's Word tells us to run from anything that stimulates youthful lusts. He tells us instead to pursue righteous living, faithfulness, love, and peace and to enjoy the companionship of those who call on the Lord with pure hearts (2 Timothy 2:22).

Let us pray:
Dear Heavenly Father, thank you for your promise that I do not suffer alone, Amen.

Verse 222

"Commit everything you do to the Lord. Trust Him, and He will help you." (Psalm 37:5)

Words for thought:

God loves us and 1 John 4:7 tells us to continue to love one another, for love comes from God and anyone who loves is a child of God and knows God. Anyone who does not love does not know God, for God is love. So loving is easy, right? Well, not exactly, because growing up in our alcoholism it created all kinds of character defects: complaining, delusion, hatred, stubborn pride, rebellion, contention, shame, guilt, disappointment, lying, despising attitudes—all of these shortcomings kept us from looking in the mirror and loving ourselves, let alone God or our fellowman. We have hope because God has given us His Spirit as proof that we live in Him and He in us (1 John 4:13). Now, let's look at the suggestion found in the Big Book of *Alcoholics Anonymous*, where it states, "See to it that your relationship with Him is right, and great events will come to pass for you and countless others. This is the great fact for us" (p. 164). Glory be to God, for there is a solution to all our drinking problems today.

Let us pray:
Dear Heavenly Father, thank you for answering my prayers, Amen.

Verse 223

"You can make many plans, but the Lord's purpose will prevail." (Proverbs 19:21)

Words for thought:

God has chosen us for a greater purpose. We may not be privy to the "why," but we are to keep the faith and be still in His presence while waiting patiently for Him to act. God wants us to seek His Kingdom above all else, and He wants us to live righteously, while He gives us everything we need (Matthew 6:33). He wants to be first in our lives and our top priority. We need to seek God honestly and openly and draw near to Him by sitting quietly, reading, praying, and listening. God has offered us a new power, a new direction to move forward while getting rid of our old self. How will we know if it is God? We will know because it will feel right, and He will gently nudge us, if we should begin drifting away from our sober path.

Let us pray:
Dear Heavenly Father, thank you for steering me straight when I begin to veer from your ways, Amen.

Verse 224

"For every house has a builder, but the one who built everything is God." (Hebrews 3:4)

Words for thought:

O nce we admitted we were powerless over alcohol, God went to work in our hearts. He waited a long time for us to come home to the truth. There is wonderful joy ahead for us as we enter our recovery journey and all those old tapes we played over and over in our thoughts will begin to lose their grip on us as we begin learning God's love. The first cornerstone to our foundation is believing in God. Knowing He is our salvation, we begin to build our trust in His Word and we receive comfort in knowing He is the truth, the way, and the life (John 4:16). So let us seek Him as our sole source of strength and believe He is the master builder of all things good to come.

Let us pray:
Dear Heavenly Father, thank you for being my healer and comforter, Amen.

Verse 225

"And so dear brothers and sisters, I plead with you to give your bodies to God because of all He has done for you. Let them be a living and holy sacrifice - the kind He will find acceptable. This is truly the way to worship Him." (Romans 12:1)

Words for thought:

Jobs, money, vacations, fears, worry, children, spouses, alcohol—these are all things of this world that kept us from putting God first in our lives. Yet, when we begin to align our will with God's will, He then sees to it that we receive His divine intervention. God wants us to be reassured that in the midst of any challenges we may face today, that we are not to be afraid, because He says, "I am the Lord, the God of all the peoples of the world. Is anything too hard for me?" (Jeremiah 32:27). God's hands will always provide for us the things that are needed. When we put that drink down that final day and we approached His throne for help, forgiveness, mercy, and guidance, and we revealed to Him our worldly sins, He simply said, "Come to me, all of you who are weary and carry heavy burdens, and I will give you rest. Take my yoke upon you. Let me teach you, because I am humble and gentle at heart, and you will find rest for your souls" (Matthew 11:28-29).

Let us pray:
Dear Heavenly Father, thank you for traveling this earth with me, Amen.

Verse 226

"Love is patient and kind. Love is not jealous or boastful or proud or rude. It does not demand its own way. It is not irritable, and it keeps no record of being wronged. It does not rejoice about injustice but rejoices whenever the truth wins out. Love never gives up, never loses faith, is always hopeful, and endures through every circumstance." (1 Corinthians 13:4-7)

Words for thought:

When we begin our day, we start by asking God to help us emulate His love toward others. Our words, actions, and thoughts are what motivates us on a daily basis and God's Word is what gives us our growth, wisdom, knowledge, discipline, gratitude, strength and assurance. His principles are perfect and they are entirely worthy of our trust. It is great news to learn God will always love us with an everlasting love! It doesn't matter what we have done or where we have been, His mercy for us will reign. The Lord has brought us out of bondage and broken every alcoholic chain that burdened us, and for that, all glory goes to Him; we cannot take credit for it. God wants us to clear our hearts of all clutter from our past, so we may love as He loves and forgive as He forgives. Let us be encouraged, because when we turn to God, He protects us and He shelters us from harm (Psalm 119:114).

Let us pray:
Dear Heavenly Father, thank you for being such an awesome God and simply loving me, Amen.

Verse 227

"Like newborn babies, you must crave pure spiritual milk so that you will grow into a full experience of salvation." (1 Peter 2:2)

Words for thought:

God already knows, in advance, that none of us here on Earth are perfect. Perfection is not a requirement of His, but growth in His Word is. In our recovery we begin to have a passion for all things that help us grow and become healthy; spiritually, emotionally, physically, mentally. So therefore we ask God to keep our desire strong in learning His ways and fruits while we humbly obey His commands.

Let us pray:
Dear Heavenly Father, thank you for the gift of maturity, Amen.

Verse 228

"Throw off your old sinful nature and your former way of life, which is corrupted by lust and deception. Instead let the Spirit renew your thoughts and attitudes." (Ephesians 4:22-23)

Words for thought:

During our days of greed and gluttony, whether it was booze, drugs, shopping, eating, gambling, or sex, we found our self-control at zero. Our morality was nowhere to be found. In fact, we lied, we stole, we abused and we cheated to get what we wanted. Satan had us right where He wanted us: demoralized. Yet, one day, God offered us a spiritual experience. He made us aware of our surrounding; He gave us insight and a God-conscious moment. In that moment, we were able to see ourselves for the first time. There was a sense of freedom and understanding to our disease. We finally were sick and tired enough to mutter, "No more, please help me," and God was there.

Let us pray:
Dear Heavenly Father, thank you for saving me from a life of further destruction, Amen.

Verse 229

*"Pray for us, for our conscience is clear and we want to
live honorably in everything we do." (Hebrews 13:18)*

Words for thought:

Honesty, open-mindedness, and willingness are the three ingredients we learn of to help us live a sober life. We can call
it the "how" of our program. It isn't until we are completely
honest with ourselves about our addiction that we could accept
help. We lived in our own world of denial, but once we entered
a program, we were able to see that our minds had shut down.
We couldn't see the devastation we were causing our family and
friends until we became open-minded to the fact that we needed
help. Then, slowly, by God's grace, we became willing. The Big
Book tells us we must go to any length to get sober. So we ask
ourselves: am I honest, open, and willing enough to get well?
Will I go to any length to achieve my goal of sobriety?

Let us pray:
*Dear Heavenly Father, thank you for giving me a daily reprieve
from my disease, Amen.*

Verse 230

So don't worry about these things, saying, "What will we eat? What will we drink? What will we wear?" These things dominate the thoughts of unbelievers, but your Heavenly Father already knows all your needs. Seek the Kingdom of God above all else, and live righteously, and He will give you everything you need. So don't worry about tomorrow, for tomorrow will bring its own worries. Today's trouble is enough for today. (Matthew 6:31-34)

Words for thought:

Did you know we could be content in all circumstances of life? Yes, if we trust in God for all our doings, He promises us fulfillment in all we do. Rest assured we will encounter trials and tribulations. However, God always provides relief in the end, and we must not quit before the miracle happens! Look at what He tells us in James 1:2-4:

Dear brothers and sisters when troubles of any kind come your way, consider it an opportunity for great joy. For you know that when your faith is tested, your endurance has a chance to grow. So let it grow, for when your endurance is fully developed, you will be perfect and complete, needing nothing.

Let us pray:

Dear Heavenly Father, thank you for carrying me when I am experiencing growth spiritually, mentally, and physically, Amen.

Verse 231

"For everyone has sinned; we all fall short of God's glorious standard." (Romans 3:23)

Words for thought:

Sin, resentment, and judgment seem to be our greatest difficulties that we choose to hold onto. Thanks be to steps four and five of the twelve steps of recovery, we do not have to continue carrying our baggage of wrongdoings and regrets forever. Confession of our shortcomings brings relief and comfort, because once we give them to God, we are forgiven; our slate is clean, so we begin to heal. Remember, God gives us free will to live a righteous life, so we must choose wisely while surrendering to His perfect plan.

Let us pray:
Dear Heavenly Father, thank you for your never-ending forgiveness when I come to you with an open heart, Amen.

Verse 232

*"I took my troubles to the Lord; I cried out to Him, and
He answered my prayer." (Psalm 120:1)*

Words for thought:

When we stepped into the realm of recovery, we didn't know who we were. Our addiction took us to persons, places, and things that were forbidding, dangerous, disturbing, frightening, and alarming. Our disease had no boundaries and it brought us to the darkest parts of our soul. However, in the midst of this turmoil of spiraling out of control, God chose to save us by His mercy, and our merciful God has made a circle of hands for us just so we may reach each other in our desperate hour. So let us come willingly and humbly before His throne to receive His glorious grace. Remembering that we take no credit for this saving, because it is only but for the grace of God, go I.

Let us pray:
Dear Heavenly Father, thank you for paving a pathway for me that leads me directly to you, Amen.

Verse 233

*"The Lord keeps you from all harm and watches over
your life. The Lord keeps watch over you as you come
and go, both now and forever." (Psalm 121:7-8)*

Words for thought:

After entering a program for our sobriety, we ask ourselves,
"Do I have clarity about my disease?" For some the answer
is "yes," but for others, the answer may be, "no." Sometimes
we overlook the spirituality of our fellowship because we are
still living in a chaotic state of mind. Step two offers us relief,
because it says, "came to believe that a power greater than ourselves could restore us to sanity." This step is the one that brings
us hope; it gives us focus. It lets us know we can longer play the
role of God. The Big Book tells us specifically on p.51: "When
many hundreds of people are able to say that the consciousness of the presence of God is today the most important fact of
their lives, they present a powerful reason why one should have
faith," so we ask ourselves, "Do I now believe, or am I willing to
believe there is a power greater than myself?" (p.47, *Alcoholics
Anonymous*). It's a direct question that needs answering for the
sake of our being "spiritually fit" or "dry drunk."

Let us pray:
*Dear Heavenly Father, I ask you in prayer, please help me
believe in my unbelief, Amen.*

Verse 234

*"A good person produces good things from the trea-
sury of a good heart, and an evil person produces evil
things from the treasury of an evil heart. What you
say flows from what is in your heart." (Luke 6:45)*

Words for thought:

A long history of our addictions has proven to harden our
hearts and hinder our maturity. It turned us into thieves,
liars, cheaters, and undependable drunks. We were mentally
and physically ill from our disease and found that we were
spiritually sick as well. We were fueled by insanity and were
dissatisfied with life. Guilt, shame, remorse, fear, depression,
anger, and resentments kept us debilitated. The Big Book says,
"Above everything, we alcoholics must be rid of the selfishness.
We must, or it kills us! God makes that possible. And there
often seems no way of entirely getting rid of self without His
aid" (p.62). At long last, we are offered a solution: a blue print
on how to live life on life's terms. Hallelujah!

Let us pray:
*Dear Heavenly Father, thank you for saving me from my own
self-destruction, Amen.*

Verse 235

"The Lord is good and does what is right; He shows the proper path to those who go astray." (Psalm 25:8)

Words for thought:

While drinking, we became so good at hiding the booze (or so we told ourselves). I'm sure we all used the excuse, "but I only had two" and sometimes we convinced ourselves of this lie, simply because we couldn't figure out "how" we got so drunk. Us drinkers thought we hid everything so well—the bottle, lies, coverups, and affairs—and for a while it all worked for us, until it didn't. Don't be discouraged; there is hope for people like us alcoholics. We can stop feeling worthless, hiding, running, and feeling all the shame from our transgressions, because God forgives us. He fills us with His promises in His Word and the word of the Lord holds true, and we can trust everything He does (Psalm 33:4). We are to embrace God's truth because we are not beyond His grace and mercy.

Let us pray:
Dear Heavenly Father, thank you that your grace is enough, Amen.

Verse 236

"The name of the Lord is a strong fortress; the godly run to Him and are safe." (Proverbs 18:10)

Words for thought:

When we enter into fellowship, we are often reminded to take our recovery slowly. We need to gently remind ourselves that for years and years, we were too sick both mentally and physically, and emotionally and spiritually. Patiently we wait on God's words, as healing does not take place overnight. When we take life one day at a time, we are not burdened with worry, because God will never ask us to carry tomorrow's burdens on today's strength.

Let us pray:
Dear Heavenly Father, thank you for the gift of life, Amen.

Verse 237

"Give all your worries and cares to God, for He cares about you." (1 Peter 5:7)

Words for thought:

Our circumstances in life can change in an instant. We look at the twenty-four hours ahead and make our plans, but what happens when our day is disrupted by something that derails us? Do we drink or do we trust God? If we have vowed to believe God in *all* things, then we know He is always with us. In fact, He is right beside us, protecting us, loving us, sheltering us. Whatever we are dealing with, we must believe God is our strength. Hallelujah!

Let us pray:
Dear Heavenly Father, thank you for being my stronghold in calmness or calamity, Amen.

Verse 238

"Don't look out only for your own interests, but take an interest in others too." (Philippians 2:4)

Words for thought:

We, the children of God, are not made to live in isolation, but that is exactly where our alcoholism landed us. We became so angry, so lonely and so frightened that we hid ourselves away from the world, thinking we had no place to turn. We surely convinced ourselves that this was the end of our time on earth. However, God offered us a light at the end of our despair. We found a program where we could get sober and learn to live life on God's terms. Our program of recovery taught us that one of the most important ingredients to our own well-being is to help the next sick and suffering alcoholic. It says to freely give away what was so generously given.

Let us pray:

Dear Heavenly Father, thank you for the many people who came before me that helped pave a way for the alcoholic, Amen.

Verse 239

*"Those who live only to satisfy their own sinful nature
will harvest decay and death from that sinful nature.
But those who live to please the Spirit will harvest
everlasting life from the spirit." (Galatians 6:8)*

Words for thought:

Steps one, two, and three releases Satan's grip on our mind,
will, and emotions. It is when we admit to our powerlessness over our alcoholism that we can become free and begin
to grow in God's guidance. Listen, God cannot do much in our
life if we continually live in denial. So thankfully, step one is
the only step that we are still in the problem, and all the others
result in our living in the solution. The steps are kind of like
a game of chess: when all its pieces are in order, then we can
make our next move and our next move is to accept who we are.
We come to realize acceptance is the key to all our problems.
We are forced to face we are no longer running the show. What
follows these two fundamental ideas is surrender. We surrender
to God's divine intervention. We become grateful He has given
us a second chance to live in freedom and we are no longer dictated by our disease.

Let us pray:
*Dear Heavenly Father, thank you for pulling me out of the gates
of hell and placing me onto solid ground, Amen.*

Verse 240

"You say, 'I am allowed to do anything' - but not everything is good for you. You say, 'I am allowed to do anything' - but not everything is beneficial. Don't be concerned for your own good but for the good of others." (1 Corinthians 10:23-24)

Words for thought:

O ur sickness made everything gloomy. We always felt tired, hurt, sad, angry, and fearful. There was no gratitude to be found in our heart. We often felt overwhelmed until our third or fourth drink kicked in and by then, we were already on our way to becoming drunk. Spouses, children, family, friends — nothing here on Earth could save us. Hell, we couldn't even save us from ourselves; we suffered from, "I sabotage myself." We needed a divine spiritual intervention. One day, the sun rose and God gave us a glimpse of hope and there was no more blaming, no more hiding, and no more running. We cried to Him, "Lord, I am sick and tired of being sick and tired." Shortly thereafter, one day at a time, we began to believe and have hope God's guidance, strength and wisdom is key to maintaining our sobriety. From there, we had work to do because the program works only if you work it!

Let us pray:
Dear Heavenly Father, thank you for giving me the saving grace to do good in your world, Amen.

Verse 241

"The lips of the godly speak helpful words, but the mouth of the wicked speaks perverse words." (Proverbs 10:32).

Words for thought:

In our drunken state, we had a fragile temperament. Our families and friends were often frightened to approach us because they were unsure of what person they would get. We were highly susceptible to fits of anger, contempt, helplessness, and sensitivity. So, it is not surprising that when we got sober, our loved ones still felt unsure of our stability. Be that as it may, we had to take action. In working steps eight and nine, we were able to show a sincere change of attitude and make our amends. Along with brotherly love and perseverance, we slowly gained back the trust which once was broken.

Let us pray:

Dear Heavenly Father, thank you for guiding my thoughts, words, and actions, Amen.

Verse 242

"Rejoice in our confident hope. Be patient in trouble, and keep on praying." (Romans 12:12)

Words for thought:

We lived so long in our illness that we believed our life was hopeless. We were in a state of utter despair. We became so disillusioned and sometimes cried out, "God, why have you forsaken me?" Then we were given light in our darkness and we experienced a tremendous relief, because we learned God never gives up on the sick and suffering alcoholic. He gives us the right to repent from our sins and turn to Him, so that all of our sins shall be wiped away (Acts 3:19). We can be encouraged today knowing when we pray, God always hears our request, and we can also believe He will give us what we ask for (1 John 5:15). God will never leave us, so we have nothing to fear when we put the drink down. One day at a time, God heals our wounds, He dries our tears, and He supplies us all the grace to live a sober life. When God offers us the guidance of the Holy Spirit, it is so we can live in His glorious fruits (Galatians 5:22-24).

Let us pray:
Dear Heavenly Father, thank you for supplying me with a brand-new self, Amen.

Verse 243

*"So do not throw away this confident trust in the Lord.
Remember the great reward it brings you! Patient
endurance is what you need now, so that you will
continue to do God's will. Then you will receive all
that he has promised." (Hebrews 10:35-36)*

Words for thought:

God has a purpose for our life. Although we wandered from His divine plan with alcoholism, it does not mean our time on Earth is finished. He knows our suffering; He knows our heart. He will help us overcome our overwhelming circumstances when we ask for His guidance. In return, He invites us to turn from the enemy and to seek His Kingdom. The Lord our God tells us in Proverbs 4:23 to guard our hearts above all else, for it determines the course of our life. We do not have to feel judged by others because we are alcoholics. We are sick people trying to get better and God alone knows our heart. We never again have to worry for God to supply what nourishes us, because His hand is plentiful for providing. His Word specifically tells us not to worry about things, saying, "What will we eat? What will we drink? What will we wear?" All these things dominate the thoughts of the unbelievers, but our Heavenly Father already knows all our needs so we are to seek the Kingdom of God above all else, and live righteously, and He will give us everything we need (Matthew 6:31-33).

Let us pray:
Dear Heavenly Father, thank you for the blessings you have granted me, Amen.

Verse 244

"Always be joyful. Never stop praying. Be thankful in all circumstances, for thus is God's will for you who belong to Christ Jesus." (1 Thessalonians 5:16)

Words for thought:

Because of our alcoholism most of our mistakes became regrets. Of course we were apologetic, but that didn't stop us from repeating them over and over again. The booze kept us in a complete cycle of lying, stealing, cheating, and manipulating and this behavior went on day after day, night after night. It was always the same old excuse: "I'll never do it again." It wasn't until we cried out and were touched by the hand of God, the spiritual awakening, that brought us into fellowship, and from there, we discovered we were not alone. See, most of our lives we felt like misfits; we just didn't belong. We knew we weren't "normal" in our thinking. We knew we couldn't continue carrying this baggage of sorrow filled with guilt, shame, and remorse because God's Word teaches us that we do not have to be enslaved to our sins anymore. We are now God's masterpiece. He created us anew in Jesus Christ's name so we can do the good things He planned for us long ago (Ephesians 2:10).

Let us pray:
Dear Heavenly Father, thank you for bringing joy back into my life, Amen.

Verse 245

"The night is almost gone; the day of salvation will soon be here. So remove your dark deeds like dirty clothes, and put on the shining armor of right living. Because we belong to the day, we must live decent lives for all to see. Don't participate in the darkness of wild parties and drunkenness, or in sexual promiscuity and immoral living, or in quarreling and jealousy. Instead, clothe yourself with the presence of the Lord Jesus Christ. And don't let yourself think about ways to indulge your evil desires."
(Romans 13:12-14)

Words for thought:

One of the most important actions we can take throughout our day is a spot-check inventory. Things like envy, selfishness, pride, greed, ego, and jealousy have a way of seeping slowly back into our subconscious. These are only some of the shortcomings we are faced with within the twenty-four hours ahead. However, this attitude only brings us pain and grief. We become fearful, angry, dissatisfied, critical, and unloving toward others. Our drink obsession returns, so do we drink, some do. Yet, we, the chosen ones, gained tools in recovery and it taught us that we can have faith, because at anytime, anywhere we can change our perspective by meditating on God's Word. It is imperative to know we can start our day over at any given moment. God grant me…

Let us pray:
Dear Heavenly Father, thank you for taking care of me, Amen.

Verse 246

"Imitate God, therefore, in everything you do, because you are His dear children." (Ephesians 5:1)

Words for thought:

Our disease has been proven year after year to be completely insidious. The book of *Alcoholics Anonymous* tells us that there are five varieties of alcoholics:

First, there is the *"emotionally unstable."*
Second, there is the *"unwilling to admit."*
Third, there is the sort that is *"free from alcohol for a period of time."*
Fourth is the *"manic depressive type."*
Fifth, some who are *"entirely normal in every respect."*

It used to be that physicians thought we were marked for death, because when we had a problem, alcohol was always our solution. If we were happy, joyous, and socializing, alcohol was the solution. We drank all the time, not like some folks who left a swig of wine behind in their fancy glass; no, never! Because of this compulsion we came to learn and accept that alcohol is an "allergy" and once we started drinking, our craving was we always wanted more, and this is because we physically lost control of choice. So we had to look back at our list and ask, "Am I number one? Two? Three? Four? Or five?"

Let us pray:
Dear Heavenly Father, thank you for helping me stay away from a drink today, Amen.

Verse 247

"This means that anyone who belongs to Christ has become a new person. The old life is gone; a new life has begun!" (2 Corinthians 5:17)

Words for thought:

In our addiction, we have lied, schemed, scammed, and deceived family members, friends, and strangers. We were so wrapped up in ourselves thinking that we were master of manipulations. The end of our drinking career was so brutal. Maybe it had to be that way because of our built-in forgetters. It is just one day, we woke up with enlightenment, and had to put a stop to the chaos, shakes, black-outs, and confusion. We took the twelve steps to God and His grace saved us. See, God had been waiting for us all along to come back to Him. He has always been our rock and redeemer, and He encourages us to take personal responsibility for ourselves, and abide in His Word. He has not given us a spirit of timidity, but of power, love, and self-discipline (2 Timothy 1:7). In the end, God saw to it that our alcoholic experience was just an end to a brand-new life. Hallelujah!

Let us pray:
Dear Heavenly Father, thank you for giving me this sober day to live, Amen.

Verse 248

"This is my command - be strong and courageous! Do not be afraid or discouraged. For the Lord your God is with you wherever you go." (Joshua 1:9)

Words for thought:

"We know that the pains of drinking had to come before sobriety and emotional turmoil before serenity" (Twelve and Twelve, p.94). Many of us have stared death right in the face at the bottom of our bottle. Our mind and body were weakened by the temptations of our flesh. We've had to ask ourselves over and over again where were we weak: in self-control, honesty, our faith, perhaps in our courage—most importantly, in our walk with God. There is a solution to our problem: God, fellowship, and abstinence. We can trust God is omniscient and offers us serenity, remembering to glorify Him, because it is His promises that always carry us through!

Let us pray:
Dear Heavenly Father, thank you for being my strength when I am weak, Amen.

Verse 249

"The eyes of the Lord watch over those who do right; His ears are open to their cries for help." (Psalm 34:15)

Words for thought:

Thanks be to God that we no longer live in fear, shame, guilt, or remorse. Once we put the drink down, our gloom began to lift from our heart and our thoughts became lucid. We were able to throw the alcoholic chains off and live the life God called us to live. There is no doubt we will still experience pain, loss and disappointments, but God's love will be strong enough in our hearts to give us comfort, peace and healing. Our restoration process will not happen overnight, simply because our program is one day at a time.

Let us pray:
Dear Heavenly Father, thank you for the big things in life you do for me, but mostly thank you for the little ones that I may miss, Amen.

Verse 250

"Yes, I am the vine; you are the branches. Those who remain in me, and I in them, will produce much fruit. For apart from me you can do nothing." (John 15:5)

Words for thought:

A dmitting to our disease was a saving grace from our Lord, because by the time we were at our lowest we had lost all hope for our future. We harbored such bitterness, anger, resentment, and fear in our minds that our hearts had become corrupt. We could no longer deny our dependency on alcohol because we compulsively had to drink. Our family and friends could only stand by the way side and watch our wreckage. As we drew nearer to God, we could feel His healing powers. We were able to put away our carousing and drunkenness and join our fellows on the "road of happy destiny" (Big Book, p.164). We learned through prayer and meditation to keep ourselves only in the day and vowed from that day forward to always give away what was so freely given to us: sobriety.

Let us pray:
Dear Heavenly Father, thank you for surrounding me with your armor of light, Amen.

Verse 251

"See, God has come to save me. I will trust in Him and not be afraid. The Lord God is my strength and my song; He has given me victory." (Isaiah 12:2)

Words for thought:

Due to our alcoholism, many of us have lost homes, jobs, cars, money, children, and spouses. We have driven drunk and sometimes had accidents that could have killed ourselves and/or others. Some have received DUIs, while still others suffered mental and physical ailments. Still, the alcoholism continued year after year with the insanity until that one moment when God offered us His saving grace. He offered us a window of clarity and a spiritual experience. Finally, we had an explanation for all the drunken mayhem in our lives and we were able to find our true selves by the grace of God. This grace is undeserved favor so we must always glorify His name.

Let us pray:
Dear Heavenly Father, thank you for bringing back from the brink of death, Amen.

Verse 252

"Come close to God, and He will come close to you.
Wash your hands, you sinners; purify your hearts, for
your loyalty is divided between God and the world."
(James 4:8)

Words for thought:

Did you know God's presence is with us wherever we are? He gifts to us the serenity that we longed for, and finally we then were able to rest. We must remember drinking only clouded our judgment. It distorted our motives. We were stuck between morality and immorality. Our character defects far outweighed the fruits of the spirit that God gives graciously. That is why we must stay the course in fellowship. We must "let go and let God." We are to remind ourselves that we are no longer the director of our own show, nor any other. This truth brings much comfort to our soul. Furthermore, we have God's Word that explains our new heart. He says:

Don't just pretend to love others. Really love them. Hate what is wrong. Hold tightly to what is good. Love each other with genuine affection, and take delight in honoring each other. Never be lazy, but work hard and serve the Lord enthusiastically. Rejoice in our confident hope. Be patient in trouble, and keep on praying. When God's people are in need, be ready to help them. Always be eager to practice hospitality. (Romans 12:9-16)

Let us pray:
Dear Heavenly Father, thank you that I no longer suffer with
my own self, Amen.

Verse 253

"I will study your commandment and reflect on your way." (Psalm 119:15)

Words for thought:

God's grace falls upon us once we let go of the wheel. Our alcoholism kept our hearts guarded against all that is good, because we felt worthless, unloved, and unwanted. We told this to ourselves in our own image in the mirror until we only had disgust for ourselves. Yet, the problem wasn't necessarily with ourselves, it was with the alcohol. We couldn't understand why we could not put down the drink. We didn't know it was the first drink that got us drunk. Then it happened—one day, God offered us a shimmer of light, He gave us a glimpse of hope. That momentary flash is what saved us, and it pointed us to freedom. The doors to recovery are open to anyone who has a "desire to stop drinking." So the problem, alcohol, finally had a solution! The solution, the recovery, the twelve steps, God, and the helping of others in our day-to-day life will ensure us we never have to drink again. Hallelujah!

Let us pray:
Dear Heavenly Father, thank you for giving me freedom from my obsession today, Amen.

Verse 254

"Now may the God of peace make you holy in every
way, and may your whole spirit and soul and body be
kept blameless until Lord Jesus Christ comes again."
(1 Thessalonians 5:23)

Words for thought:

We wondered to ourselves for many years if we will ever again experience life free of the agony of being drunk. We knew something was wrong, and we kept searching for a way out. Day after day, we awoke with repeated apologize and broken promises to our loved ones. We didn't know life sober until we were touched by the hand of God. There is no other explanation, because our minds were crushed, exhausted, and impaired, but our hearts felt hopeful. Something changed. We became willing to give this sober thing a try, and through God, fellow members, and meetings, we put the drink at bay, for today!

Let us pray:
Dear Heavenly Father, thank you for a way out of my alcoholic
misery, Amen.

Verse 255

"Hatred stirs up conflict, but love covers all wrongs."
(Proverbs 10:12)

Words for thought:

If we remove hate and anger, what is left is God's love. If we remove anxiety and fear, serenity will result. If we believe in God's promises, then the obstacles that we created between God and ourselves will vanish. With these shortcomings removed, we begin to be an instrument of God's fruits. (Galatians 5:22-23). We clearly have been touched by the hand of God and He has done His part, but now we must do ours. The Lord will continue to heal us mentally, physically, and spiritually as we speak of all the good things He has done. Let us praise Him, because His unfailing love is better than life itself. (Psalm 63:3)

Let us pray:
Dear Heavenly Father, you know my heart and my struggles I pray you lighten my burdens today, Amen.

Verse 256

"Anyone who listens to my teaching and follows it is wise, like a person who builds a house on solid rock." (Matthew 7:24)

Words for thought:

O nce we started to build our foundation on God's Word, we came to believe we have been made anew. We no longer refuse to face reality. We made a decision to put the drink down and follow a few simple rules. With each new day, we found courage and hope as God's presence became stronger in our hearts. We came to His altar when we walked through the doors of recovery. Only God lifted our suffering and gave us hope; He saved us! Our old behaviors He swept clean and with daily inventory we remain strong and immovable. As we go through our twenty-four hours, we are to meditate and give all the glory back to God. So, when we live for the Lord, we will surely be a blessing to the next sick and suffering who walks through the doors.

Let us pray:
Dear Heavenly Father, thank you for giving me the joy to live life, Amen.

Verse 257

"This means that anyone who belongs to Christ has become a new person. The old life is gone; a new life has begun. And all of this is a gift from God, who brought us back to himself through Christ. And God has given us this task of reconciling people to Him."
(2 Corinthians 5:17-18)

Words for thought:

Once in recovery, we give God all the control, because we've tried our own way for much too long, and our suffering has been great. It is miraculous how God led us in a direction away from the drunken shell of a person with a lifeless soul we had become. He encourages us to hold onto Him in the middle of the storm, but to remain patient while He brings us through. God is magnificent and He teaches us humility, gratitude, forgiveness, and love. Remember, God knows our story, yet He doesn't stay angry at us forever, as people do. God has compassion and unfailing love for us. He wants us to live in peace with joy, love, songs, and laughter, together!

Let us pray:
Dear Heavenly Father, thank you for being an incredible light through all of my darkness, Amen.

Verse 258

"Teach me your ways, O Lord, that I may live according to your truth." (Psalm 86:11)

Words for thought:

B oy, have we made mistakes! In our defense, when we began our partying years, we were not made aware of becoming an *alcoholic*! Now it's time to grow up, but John Barleycorn has a different direction and that's when our allergy to alcohol starting seeping through our veins. Then years and years pass us by before our denial begins to lift. Our eyes become open to see the destruction we caused in our own homes and with our relationships, and for the first time, we feel the presence of God. This time, God's pull is stronger than before. We suddenly believe our alcoholism is the problem and not the solution, so we must cease indulging. God wants us to be right in His eye. He wants our repentance, so He can forgive us and love us through all our self-inflicted pain. Now God wants to give us a new direction to follow. He wants us to have obedience to His Word and accountability for our actions. We do not have to navigate through this world alone, because the Lord offers us His salvation, and He guides us so others may see Him through our ways.

Let us pray:
Dear Heavenly Father, thank you for redeeming me and setting me free from bondage of self, Amen.

Verse 259

"The Lord is merciful and compassionate, slow to get angry and filled with unfailing love." (Psalm 145:8)

Words for thought:

So often we think God is mad at us because of how much alcohol we consumed and how drunk we became on a daily basis. We felt we had no privilege to go before Him because of the pain and suffering we caused ourselves and our loved ones. We felt unworthy of His love because our disease told us so. Satan whispered in our ear day after day, "God can't save you. You are nothing. You're worthless. You're better off dead." But lo and behold, we came to believe in the real truth. Matthew 16:23 says, "Get away from me Satan! You are a dangerous trap to me. You are seeing things from a human point of view, not from God's." So therefore this offers us a chance to think, think, think before we pick up that first drink. We are to receive God's love right where we are—yes, right in the middle of our addiction.

Let us pray:

Dear Heavenly Father, thank you for reaching down and plucking me out of the hands of Satan, Amen.

Verse 260

*"When I was a child, I spoke and thought and rea-
soned as a child. But when I grew up, I put away
childish things." (1 Corinthians 13:11)*

Words for thought:

Not many of us want to admit our faults. Furthermore, none of us wants to believe, although we are grown-ups, we act as mature as the five-year-old child inside us. Alcohol stole many years from us. It took away some of the most precious people and things in our lives. While the world continued around us, we became desensitized in the bottle. However, through all the disarray, God offered us a way out. He told us, "Come to me, all of you who are weary and carry heavy burdens, and I will give you rest" (Matthew 11:28). When we finally take step three, our lives will be on solid ground. It may still be a bit shaky for the first ninety days, but once God's hand starts building that foundation and we continue working the twelve steps with Him, then all the promises of recovery will begin to materialize. Hallelujah!

Let us pray:
Dear Heavenly Father, thank you for protecting me while I was on my path of destruction, Amen.

Verse 261

*"Let each generation tell its children of your mighty
acts; let them proclaim your power." (Psalm 145:4)*

Words for thought:

We alcoholics who are fortunate enough to find "the rooms"
know the importance of building a solid spiritual foundation. In fact, the Big Book tells us in two of its chapters: "It has
been repeatedly proven among us that upon this simple cornerstone a wonderfully effective spiritual structure can be built"
(p. 47). Moving forward, p.75 asks us, "Is our work solid so
far? Are the stones properly in place? Have we skimped on the
cement put into the foundation? Have we tried to make mortar
without sand?" Fellow members, we have no room for reserva-
tions. Our solid rock is God, but if we begin to lose faith, our
whole structure will come tumbling down. So let us live each
twenty-four hours with God and for God so we may receive our
daily reprieve. So what is next for us? Action! Action! Action!

Let us pray:
*Dear Heavenly Father, thank you for permitting me to build my
house on your Word, Amen.*

Verse 262

"God is our refuge and strength, always ready to help in times of trouble." (Psalm 46:1)

Words for thought:

It used to be that we had to start our day with a glass of liquor. We begged and we pleaded with ourselves not to pick up that first drink. Yet, our heads were foggy, our thoughts jumbled, our hands shaky, and our bodies sick. We needed a divine intervention. So in a moment of clarity, we were finally able to acknowledge God has been waiting for us, and once we were honest with Him and ourselves, He could then deliver us from our obsession. God is able to lift us from complete insanity and deliver us to soundness of mind, but we have a part to play. So at the beginning of a new day, we seek Him first, and ask Him to give us direction for the day. As we learn God's Word, we will be able to stand firm against the enemy and His temptation of drink will simply be washed away.

Let us pray:
Dear Heavenly Father, thank you for guiding me on a sober path today, Amen.

Verse 263

"Love the Lord your God with all your heart, and with all your soul, and with all your strength." (Deuteronomy 6:5)

Words for thought:

When we pray, we have to ask God for those things that will help us grow. Daily, we ask Him for guidance in love, knowledge, and understanding of others. We pray for acceptance because it truly is the key to life. Throughout our day, we are to look for moments that give us an opportunity to do good for others. Remember, God loves us and cares about our inner beings. Wherever we go, God is with us and our life should reflect the love we have for Him.

Let us pray:
Dear Heavenly Father, thank you for my hope and courage. Thank you for loving me first, Amen.

Verse 264

*"God saved you by His grace when you believed. And
you can't take credit for this; it is a gift from God."
(Ephesians 2:8)*

Words for thought:

We had this dreadful feeling that someone was always mad at us. It wasn't necessarily true, but let's face it—for years we were awakened with complete and utter amnesia of what scene we caused the night before. We got to the point in our drunkenness that we didn't even try to save face, and by the end of the night, we were literally looking out of one eye, and when that didn't work, we simply passed out. And guess what? We did it all over again the next day! Yet, on one of those days, our heart was willing to make a change, and at once, our minds aligned with the truth, and in that brief moment, we experienced God. We finally admitted to our alcoholism. We finally found the solution to our drinking problem. We finally learned how not to play Dr. Jekyll and Mr. Hyde. We are encouraged by God's Word not to be impressed by our own wisdom, but instead fear the Lord and turn from the world's evil because then we will have healing for our bodies and strength for our bones (Proverbs 3:7).

Let us pray:
Dear Heavenly Father, thank you for guiding my path to a life that you have given me, Amen.

Verse 265

"Since He Himself has gone through suffering and testing, He is able to help us when we are being tested." (Hebrews 2:18)

Words for thought:

We need to let our life be defined by God, for if we allow the world to define us, we will live in complete turmoil and chaos. This earth is full of all kinds of evil. Satan causes disorder and immorality of all kinds and keeps them hidden in the shadows. He wanted us trapped in the bottle. He used this temptation to bring us into hell. He wanted us to lose all enjoyment in our families, workplace, hobbies, and interests. He created distractions and illusions to keep us from our true selves. He wants to keep us thirsty for our alcohol, but not God. In Matthew 6:33, it states, "Seek the kingdom of God above all else, and live righteously, and He will give you everything you need." We need to take notice, because this says everything we "need" not everything we "want" and Satan will use this to take advantage of our circumstances. So this encourages us to remain spiritually fit and to arm ourselves with God's armor of truth, so we will not leave the door ajar to Satan's tactics.

Let us pray:
Dear Heavenly Father, thank you that I have the privilege to worship your Holy name, Amen.

Verse 266

"O Lord, I have come to you for protection; don't let
me be disgraced. Save me, for you do what is right.
Turn your ear to listen to me; rescue me quickly be
my rock of protection, a fortress where I will be safe."
(Psalm 31:1-2)

Words for thought:

O God, we cried out your name and we heard your voice so we prayed, "Please forgive us." You allowed a new day to dawn and because of your mercy, we've been saved. We prayed to your holy name and you gave us peace. Our obsession with alcohol was lifted from us, and we are no longer shackled to the bottle. You have given us a new spirit and you said to fill it with love and to spread the good news of our experience, strength, and hope to any newcomer that comes our way.

Let us pray:
Dear Heavenly Father, thank you for granting me the grace to become a sober person today, Amen.

Verse 267

*My child, listen to me and do as I say, and you will
have a long, good life. I will teach you wisdom's ways
and lead you in straight paths. When you walk, you
won't be held back; when you run, you won't stumble.
Take hold of my instructions; don't let them go. Guard
them, for they are the key to life. (Proverbs 4:10-13)*

Words for thought:

M any of us come into the program so sick and so beaten down
that we have no faith there is a God. We asked, if there is a
God who reigns over all, then how could He ever allow this to
happen to us? We soon learn, however, that this ruination was
of our own making. Our whole mental state was blurred from
the drink and our outlook and perspective were askew. After
joining fellowship, we began to learn we are not alone. We
slowly started to figure it out, and with the twelve steps in our
back pocket, we started setting aside old images and mistaken
beliefs about God, and allowed Him the time to restore us to
sanity. True humility, an open mind, and complete willingness
is the key to our faith, and us loving God and keeping His commandments only proves our love for Him.

Let us pray:
Dear Heavenly Father, thank you for loving me, Amen.

Verse 268

"Come and listen to my counsel. I'll share my heart with you and make you wise." (Proverbs 1:23)

Words for thought:

One of the suggestions from our program is to change our persons, places, and things. Becoming sober means we move forward from our past, humbly thanking God for His forgiveness. We're not saying this makes us better than our old drinking pals, it means we need to grow and move in a different direction, a clean way of living. There is a season, a reason, and a lifetime for all things. When God calls us, it is time for us to just listen, and then rise above our circumstance. Our sober goal is to want to please God, and not man. The reward we receive when we do this is that we leave zero room for regret!

Let us pray:
Dear Heavenly Father, thank you for guiding me with your instructions, Amen.

Verse 269

*"Leave your simple ways behind, and begin to live;
learn to use good judgment." (Proverbs 9:6)*

Words for thought:

D ual addiction is widespread in today's society. People end up in jail, institutionalized, or dead. However, we no longer need to live with the pain and suffering from our disease. There is a way of recovery that has been paved for us long ago. If we decisively choose to say no to any form of addiction and find God, our life will be worth living again. At some point, we grow up and leave our childish ways behind. God's Word enriches our thinking and we begin to have hope that we can clean house, make amends, spread the news, and live one day at a time. So come join us as we "trudge the road of happy destiny" (p.164, Big Book).

Let us pray:
Dear Heavenly Father, thank you for granting me the bravery to live for the day, Amen.

Verse 270

"For God is working in you giving you the desire and the power to do what pleases Him." (Philippians 2:13)

Words for thought:

When we pray, we should remember to petition for those things God has planned for us. We pray for His will and not our own selfish desires. Let us not ask for any reward that will fill our own pride. Let us only live by God's Word and His blessings will be abundant.

Let us pray:
Dear Heavenly Father, thank you in advance for all the blessings this day will bring. Bring peace to those in need today Lord, Amen.

Verse 271

"Fools think their own way is right, but the wise listen to others." (Proverbs 12:15)

Words for thought:

Before coming into the program, our drunken emotions dictated how we would feel for that day. We were sometimes sad, angry, depressed, lonely, intolerant, guilty, shameful, irritated, indignant, happy, resentful, loving. We were like a rollercoaster that never stopped at its landing. However, the great news is in God's Word, because His Word is never changing. It doesn't stop and go, or go side to side, because He is our anchor. His Word is always clear, concise, consistent, and concrete. So for today, my friends, let us enjoy our sobriety while seeking God's will in all we do.

Let us pray:
Dear Heavenly Father, thank you for steadying my walk with you, Amen.

Verse 272

"Trust in the Lord and do good. Then you will live safely in the land and prosper. Take delight in the Lord, and He will give you your hearts desires." (Psalm 37:3-4)

Words for thought:

Our alcoholic days of being drunk always left us open to an attack. We allowed ourselves to be vulnerable to the lies of Satan. He captured every thought that would come into our mind, and he twisted and he turned those thoughts. Satan made us defenseless to the evils of this world. Yet, once we committed ourselves to sobriety and the Word of God, we could then breathe a sigh of relief. God could finally bring us to a place of renewing of our mind. He gave us peace, comfort, and healing. He granted us love, joy, and happiness. God promises He will give us all the strength, courage, and wisdom we need to live a sober life, one day at a time. He delivered us from our alcoholism so we in return can glorify His name.

Let us pray:
Dear Heavenly Father, thank you for this precious gift of sobriety, Amen.

Verse 273

"My child, never forget the things I have taught you.
Store my commands in your heart. If you do this, you
will live many years, and your life will be satisfying."
(Proverbs 3:1-2)

Words for thought:

Drinking used to be fun. Growing up with alcohol seemed like an easy life. It gave us courage. It made us bolder. It gave us confidence. It lowered our inhibitions. It allowed us to feel prettier or more handsome. It allowed us to be flirtatious, even promiscuous. Liquor eventually, however, let us make promises we couldn't keep. Appointments we didn't show up for. Dates that were ruined. It caused car wrecks, jail time, hospital stays, and DUIs. It enabled us to do things we normally wouldn't do, and go places we normally wouldn't go. Alcohol used to be our friend; until it wasn't. We asked ourselves over and over again, "How did I get this bad?" The good news is God gives us the courage to change. We need not fear change nor be anxious over it, because it is a guarantee in life that it will happen, but what we do is gain the wisdom to know the difference. Believe in God's steadfast love He has stored up because He knows our heart and He listens on purpose. In Psalm 32:8, He assures us that He will guide us along the best pathway for our life. Hallelujah!

Let us pray:
Dear Heavenly Father, thank you for being all powerful and all knowing, Amen.

Verse 274

"It is pleasant to see dreams come true, but fools refuse to turn from evil to attain it." (Proverbs 3:19)

Words for thought:

Our alcoholism has caused us to feel underpowered in so many areas of our life. We lost total control of making simple decisions for ourselves. We became unwelcomed, unloved, and undeserving by many who once stood by our side, but yet we were convinced that it was all their fault. Our disease tells us that we do not have a sickness, so our ears have been closed off from any good counsel or godly wisdom. Many of us hit rock bottom before we could admit, accept, and surrender to needing help. Through a spiritual awakening, we slowly put away our pride and ego. We finally made a decision, then slowly we came to believe in the power of God and through faith we began to gain hope for ourselves, and our family. Because of God, we graciously learned to live life one day at a time.

Let us pray:
Dear Heavenly Father, thank you for giving me one moment in my life that helped save me from myself, Amen.

Verse 275

There are different kinds of spiritual gifts, but the same Spirit is the source of them all. There are different kinds of service, but we serve the same Lord. God works in different ways, but it is the same God who does the work for all of us. A spiritual gift is given to each of us so we can help each other. (1 Corinthians 12:4-7)

Words for thought:

God gives us a daily reprieve to our inner thirst for alcohol. He gives us a way out of our darkness and directs us to the path of light we must follow. God gives us strength to endure our disease and not to escape it. In Matthew 6:33, God promises to give us, "Everything we need"—all the food, drink, shelter, transportation, clothing, all the financial means and education—but first we must "seek the kingdom of God above all else." We are to glorify His righteous name and walk the good life of sobriety, and all these things will be added onto us. Remember, we do not earn salvation on our own merits, but by the grace of our Jesus Christ.

Let us pray:
Dear Heavenly Father, thank you for being the merciful God who can do all things, Amen.

Verse 276

Put on all of God's armor so that you will be able to stand firm against all strategies of the devil. For we are not fighting against flesh-and-blood enemies, but against evil rulers and authorities of the unseen world, against mighty powers in this dark world, and against evil spirits in the heavenly places. (Ephesians 6:11-12)

Words for thought:

We often asked ourselves why we sat with Satan for so long. Why did we miss out on so many years of our lives because of our alcoholism? Why did we choose to chat with evil when we knew He only came to "kill, steal, and destroy" our life? We were in mental agony with our disease and we thought for so long that we were losing our sanity. Satan loved the insanity knowing we would do the same thing day after day, over and over again. However, one day we woke and had this moment of lucidity. We spoke out loud of our pain and suffering and God heard our cries. At that moment, we allowed Him into our hearts and that is when He began to move mountains in our sobriety. In His hands, we have it all: His Word, promises, love, and harmony. Hallelujah!

Let us pray:
Dear Heavenly Father, thank you for giving me proof of your love, Amen.

Verse 277

*"I will praise you with all my heart, O Lord my God;
I will proclaim your greatness forever. How great is
your constant love for me! You have saved me from
the grave itself." (Psalm 86:12-13)*

Words for thought:

We never felt as alone as we did in the bottom of the bottle. In the end, we isolated ourselves because we wanted to get drunk. We had to reach that level of numbing ourselves. We didn't know why; we started out with good intention, we just wanted to take the edge off. That didn't work, because the next thing we knew, we woke up to the torment of what we did, wondering if it was still even today. We cried out many times for God to hear us, but this day was different, because we were lead to our program of recovery and slowly, we were able to see God's instructions were straightforward. There were no gimmicks, no lies, just God and His Word. Having this new safe haven in God and applying the twelve steps of recovery to our daily living brings us to serving others and this we can be grateful for!

Let us pray:
Dear Heavenly Father, thank you for the promises that are in your word, Amen.

Verse 278

"Wherever your treasure is, there the desires of your heart will also be." (Matthew 6:21)

Words for thought:

Sometimes life is just too damn hard. The nights are long and the days gloomy. Even if it was a beautiful day, in the end we only wanted darkness, for we just could not bear another drunk day. The turmoil and confusion, the homicidal and suicidal thoughts that crossed our minds while intoxicated was a frightening way to live, think, and feel. This merry-go-round of alcoholism had to stop, and so it did. We were offered a solution, a program to follow, a brand-new life through the Holy Spirit. We learned to love, trust, and have faith in God and ourselves. We learned about selflessness, gratitude, and forgiveness. The Apostle Paul in Romans 12 pleads with us to give our bodies to God for all He has done for us. We are to let them be a Holy sacrifice to Him. He says this is truly a way to worship God. So let us keep the discipline to start each brand-new day listening to God first.

Let us pray:
Dear Heavenly Father, thank you that I never again have to walk this road alone, Amen.

Verse 279

*"You haven't done this before. Ask, using my name,
and you will receive, and will have abundant joy."
(John 16:24)*

Words for thought:

God's instructions are sometimes firm and demanding, but this is only because God has a great love for us. He came to us when we were at our lowest point: confused, intoxicated, and emotionally bankrupt. He came to give us guidance, healing, forgiveness, purpose, focus, and discipline. God did not give us a spirit of fear and timidity, but of power, love, and self-discipline (2 Timothy 1:7). Step three tells us to make a decision. We have to decide whether God is or isn't going to be our first priority. It is written, "When we became alcoholic, crushed by a self-imposed crisis we could not postpone or evade, we had to fearlessly face the proposition that either God is everything or else He is nothing" (p.53, The Big Book). The Lord our God tells us, "I am the Alpha and Omega, the beginning and the end. I am the one who is, who always was, and who is still to come, the Almighty One" (Revelation 1:8).

Let us pray:
Dear Heavenly Father, thank you for granting me the choice of free will to believe, Amen.

Verse 280

"And don't forget to do good and to share with those in need. These are the sacrifices that please God."
(Hebrews 13:16)

Words for thought:

The drink, overtime, takes our self-worth and dignity. Our morals suffer and we get knocked down and can't get back up. Some of us survive this disease while others either end up institutionalized, in jail, or dead. Some people just cannot get the program of recovery and for some they can't or won't accept the spiritual aspect of God in their lives, therefore they have no defense against the first drink. So we ask ourselves: where am I on my journey with God? Do I have rigorous honesty? Am I helping the next sick and suffering who walks through the doors of AA? Am I willing to go to any length to remain sober? The Big Book tells us to "abandon yourself to God as you understand God" (p.164). All we have to do is ask Him to help us set aside all the things we thought we knew so we have an open mind for a new life sober. Folks, we are gifted in this program of recovery. We get to live two lifetimes—one drunk and one sober—so remember, "I can't, He can, so let Him."

Let us pray:
Dear Heavenly Father, thank you for only requiring progress and not perfection from me, Amen.

Verse 281

*"Those who only live to satisfy their own sinful nature
will harvest decay and death from that sinful nature.
But those who live to please the Spirit will harvest
everlasting life from the Spirit." (Galatians 6:8)*

Words for thought:

G od is the strength of our soul. Yet, we clouded our mind, heart, and any good judgment we had for ourselves with greed, gluttony, lust, pride, sloth, wrath, and envy. We chose to hate instead of love. We chose misery over joy. We chose alcohol over life. We lived in complete despair until we surrendered to God, and once we allowed Him to flow through our hearts, we were convinced nothing can separate us from His love. Not death or life, angels or demons, not even our fears for today or any worries of tomorrow can keep us from Him. It says not even the powers of hell can come between us and God's love. The Apostle Paul further states not even the power in the sky above nor on Earth can separate us. Nothing in all creation will ever be able to divide us from the love of God that is revealed in Jesus Christ our Lord (Romans 8:38-39).

Let us pray:
Dear Heavenly Father, thank you for bringing me to a better place and guiding me to the truth, Amen.

Verse 282

"He lifted me out of the pit of despair, out of the mud and the mire. He set my feet on solid ground and steadied me as I walked along." (Psalm 40:2)

Words for thought:

No matter where we've been, God has always been there. Our drunkenness is not of God's making, but of our own destructive behavior. We stumbled through life with a drink in hand for weeks, months, and years. We became so lost that we couldn't see our way through the storm. We knew we should not drink, but the thought of never drinking again just kept us drunk longer. We could not live in this pit of despair another day. Then, in this state of consciousness we experienced a change, a shift in attitude, something telling us we wanted more than that drink, and we sought help in the rooms. We listened, we shared, we spilled our lives to God and another, and we learned it is only one day at a time. So let us continue our journey and as we go along, remember God is only as far away as this prayer, "Search me O God, and know my anxious thoughts. Point out anything in me that offends you, and lead me along the path of everlasting life" (Psalm 139:23-24).

Let us pray:
Dear Heavenly Father, thank you for lifting my gloom, Amen.

Verse 283

So be careful how you live. Don't live like fools, but like those who are wise. Make the most of every opportunity in these evil days. Don't act thoughtlessly, but understand what the Lord wants you to do. Don't be drunk with wine, because that will ruin your life. Instead, be filled with the Holy Spirit. (Ephesians 5:15-18)

Words for thought:

Our life has many twists and turns that God uses to make us who we are today. There are many illnesses in this world and ours is alcoholism. A disease so cunning, baffling, and powerful that it affects us mentally, physically, and spiritually. The one question we always ask ourselves is: were we born alcoholic or did our circumstances make us alcoholics? God gave us all a story and then He gave us free will to live that life. Some rode that life happy and free from the bondage of self, but not us, because we have a disease. However at some point, we came to discover we were not alone. There are millions of people just like us and what a miracle, because together we help each other; one alcoholic talking to another sharing our experience, strength, and hope. God gave us an answer to our malady. It is a program of recovery and it is available to all of us and anyone who has the desire to stop drinking.

Let us pray:
Dear Heavenly Father, thank you that you have blessed us with a solution to our illness, Amen.

Verse 284

"But those who trust in the Lord will find new strength. They will soar high on wings like eagles. They will run and not grow weary. They will walk and not faint." (Isaiah 40:31)

Words for thought:

O ur alcoholism was like a hurricane with its flooding waters and destructive winds. It tore at our core and ripped apart our world. Our foundation cracked and our footsteps continually fell into its crevices. We were unsteady and unstable on our feet until we were so sickened by our disease that we at long last reached out for help, and God was there when we fell to our knees. It is made clear in this message of Galatians 5 that when we follow the desires of our sinful nature, the results are clear: there is sexual immorality, impurity, lustful measures, idolatry, sorcery, hostility, quarreling, jealousy, outbursts of anger, selfish ambition, dissension, division, envy, drunkenness, wild parties, and other sins like these. If we choose these things, we will not inherit the kingdom of God. He tells us to get rid of anger, rage, malice, slander, and filthy language from our lips (Colossians 3:8) and in a sober mind, we are capable of hearing God's voice. We are capable to follow God's direction, but are we of the disciplined type? God showed us we are not alone in our tragic aloneness. So He gave us a new life, a simple program, and each other. Hallelujah!

Let us pray:
Dear Heavenly Father, thank you for allowing me to hear your voice above all others, Amen.

Verse 285

"Pray in the spirit at all times and on every occasion. Stay alert and be persistent in your prayers for all believers everywhere." (Ephesians 6:18)

Words for thought:

In our denial, we did not want to believe, nor did we want to take accountability that alcohol was our problem. Our life experiences were met with bitterness, jealousy, anger, and sadness. Our minds were captive to anxiety, doubt, fear, and worry. We created all kinds of torment, pain, and suffering to our loved ones. Then, one day, we took a long look in the mirror at ourselves and realized we couldn't go on with our alcoholic torture one more day. We knew we needed help beyond human aid and our program taught us that we were no longer fighting just a physical battle, but a spiritual one too. It is important for us to believe God wants us to know He will connect with us right where we are: humble and broken.

Let us pray:
Dear Heavenly Father, thank you for being my refuge and only hope, Amen.

Verse 286

"And remember, when you are being tempted, do not say, 'God is tempting me.' God is never tempted to do wrong, and He never tempts anyone else. Temptation comes from our own desires, which entice us and drag us away." (James 1:13-14)

Words for thought:

Does it matter how we came to God as long as we finally arrived at His doorstep? No, it does not! See, He already knew we were beaten and battered and full of self, but it says, "Come to me all who labor and are heavy laden, and I will give you rest" (Matthew 11:28). Let us come boldly to God and ask Him to give us strength when we are weak, because the temptations of this world are strong and the biggest temptation we face is not to pick up that first drink today. Let us pray that our thoughts and actions are pure so we may remain close to God. We must remember when we are deeply rooted in prayer and we continually seek God's wisdom and guidance, we can be reassured He will protect us against the seduction of alcohol and its mouthwatering appeal.

Let us pray:
Dear Heavenly Father, thank you for giving me your Word so I may build my foundation upon you, Amen.

Verse 287

"O Lord, do not stay far away! You are my strength;
come quickly to my aid!" (Psalm 22:19)

Words for thought:

In our past we have all had some kind of experience that has brought us sorrow. The average person embraced their heartache and allowed God to heal their pain. But not us, the alcoholic—we took this distress as another way to get all boozed up. Therefore we never went through the grieving process, but stuffed it deep down only to be brought out at a later date. This gave us a reason to get drunk all over again. It is the insanity of our thinking and drinking—doing the same thing over and over again expecting different results. However, we then discovered a power greater than ourselves and we started to believe God doesn't give us anything that we cannot handle. We believe His promises empower us to walk through the suffering, in a sober mind, with Him. So, let our glory be to God, for He is good!

Let us pray:
Dear Heavenly Father, thank you for being my guiding light through all my dark days, Amen.

Verse 288

"Love never gives up, never loses faith, is always hopeful, and endures through every circumstance." (1 Corinthians 13:7)

Words for thought:

During our drinking, we felt undeserving of God's grace. We soon learned in our program of recovery that God does not hold against us our sins. Although we may be discouraged or unsure of where God is taking us, we can have faith that He will never leave us alone. Even when we isolate with shades drawn, phone on vibrate, He refuses to leave us. He kept us close to Him and He waited patiently for us to come to surrender our will to Him. When we were willing, God began filling our heart with hope, love, gratitude, purity, unselfishness, honesty, and discipline. Now we go and help the next fellow member who reaches out for help.

Let us pray:

Dear Heavenly Father, thank you because all I have to do is ask and I receive, Amen.

Verse 289

"Many people say, 'Who will show us better times?'
Let your face shine on us, Lord. You have given me
greater joy than those who have abundant harvests
of grain and new wine. In peace I will lie down and
sleep, for you alone, O Lord, will keep me safe."
(Psalm 4:6-8)

Words for thought:

Alcohol was fun, until it wasn't, and when it became our dirty little secret it took on a life all of its own. This is when the selfishness and self-centered defects began. This is when the lying, stealing, cheating, and fear started to consume our lives. The alcohol became this giant that we thought could never be defeated. We had to find a way to neutralize our disease of alcoholism and we had to identify all these obstacles that stood in our way, which kept us from loving life and living it joyfully. We had to gather all the strength and courage we could manage and turn our lives over to the care of God, so we could live one day at a time, free from our obsession. As David did to Goliath, we too had to take down this giant in our lives. Hallelujah!

Let us pray:
Dear Heavenly Father, thank you for changing my life one day at a time, Amen.

Verse 290

"Teach me your decrees, O Lord; I will keep them to the end. Give me understanding and I will obey your instructions; I will put them into practice with all my heart. Make me walk along the path of your commands, for that is where my happiness is found."
(Psalm 119:33-35)

Words for thought:

A lcohol confused our mind. It held us captive against our own will. It took our emotions and turned them into turmoil. Our future was bleak and many of us thought death was our only option. Day after day, we allowed our moods and personal circumstances to dictate how we were going to get through the day. We drank because we did not have soundness of mind. The insanity was so overwhelming that we began to drink ourselves to death. We didn't know we needed a complete change until we were offered a place of healing. With God, the rooms of recovery, and a blueprint of the twelve steps, we are offered a life, free of alcohol, one day at a time as long as we stay open, honest, willing, and disciplined to work at it! So are you?

Let us pray:
Dear Heavenly Father, thank you that I no longer have to suffer inside my own head, Amen.

Verse 291

"You who love the Lord, hate evil! He protects the lives of His godly people and rescues them from the power of the wicked. Light shines on the godly, and joy on those whose hearts are right." (Psalm 97:10-11)

Words of thought:

It's a funny thing about life—everything can be normal and then in a minute it can all turn upside down. No one escapes this world unscathed and unfortunately for us alcoholics, we bring forth some of these burdens upon ourselves. However, the truth of the matter is this: we have an illness, a disease, that attacks us the minute we put a drink to our lips. The allergy that attacks us is physically, emotionally, and spiritually damaging, and once our compulsion begins, we no longer have the willpower to fend it off. There is no magic spell for our malady, but there is one of influence, and that one is God. See, Satan intended liquor to be our ultimate end, but God, He intervened and turned our disgraceful obsession into something magnificent that changes our lives forever, all so we may glorify His name.

Let us pray:

Dear Heavenly Father, thank you for turning my life into something worth living again, Amen.

Verse 292

*"Help me understand the meaning of your command-
ments, and I will meditate on your wonderful deeds.
I weep with sorrow; encourage me by your word.
Keep me from lying to myself; give me the privilege
of knowing your instructions." (Psalm 119:27-29)*

Words for thought:

As far back as many of us can remember, our minds were
twisted. We felt alone in our own world—that is, until we
found liquor. Most of us agree our alcoholism took flight in our
preteen years. We grew to become inpatient, intolerant, mean,
and egotistical. We had no use for those whose views or behaviors differed from our own, and what we did was isolate ourselves from the ones who loved us the most. Whether we choose
to believe it or not, these loved ones prayed us, and then came
the day God offered us an olive branch, and it was our road to
recovery. However, were we wise enough to take it? The answer
is yes, for some. Unfortunately, not all will be joining us on our
journey to a happy and sober day. Remember, but for the grace
of God, go I.

Let us pray:
*Dear Heavenly Father, thank you for giving me a fellowship
that healed me from the inside out, Amen.*

Verse 293

"Now all glory to God, who is able, through His mighty power at work within us, to accomplish infinitely more than we might ask or think." (Ephesians 3:20)

Words for thought:

All of our actions and behaviors have consequences, some good, some bad, but one thing for sure: we learn from all of them. While drinking, our minds were cluttered and confused. Our big ideas seemed great while we were drunk, but most of the time they were disastrous. There were the friends who threw their hands up in defeat. There were family members who simply walked away. Then there were spouses and children who lived in distress and misfortune while we drank our days away. They could not rescue us, but by an act of God, we were saved, and eventually our families were mended. God brought us to AA so we can gather in fellowship and help one another by spreading the good news of our experience, strength, and hope.

Let us pray:
Dear Heavenly Father, thank you for rescuing and mending me back to health, Amen.

Verse 294

"For the Lord grants wisdom! From His mouth come knowledge and understanding. He grants a treasure of common sense to the honest. He is a shield to those who walk with integrity. He guards the paths of the just and protects those who are faithful to Him."
(Proverbs 2:6-8)

Words for thought:

We are a sick variety of individuals from the disease of alcoholism. We chose for years and years to live in denial of our drinking. We tried to convince ourselves and others that we could stop at any time. We tried to control what time our drinking would begin because we swore it would never be morning time. We also tried switching the type of booze we drank, thinking one got us less drunk than the other. We even tried just having two and failed miserably at that because our compulsion outweighed any logical thinking. Hell, the bar we set for ourselves just kept getting lower and lower until we hit bottom. Once there, we came to realize we needed help. We discovered we had to have clarity to move forward. We learned how to live one day at a time and we learned to let God take the wheel. Most importantly, we gained insight on the meaning of abstinence and working our twelve-step program.

Let us pray:
Dear Heavenly Father, thank you for granting me the wisdom to knowing the difference between the things I can and the things I cannot change, Amen.

Verse 295

"And we are confident that He hears us whenever we ask for anything that pleases Him. And since we know He hears us when we make our requests, we also know that He will give us what we ask." (1 John 5:14-15)

Words for thought:

Alcohol makes our lives tumble down before us and we eventually cannot recognize the truth from our own lies. It caused us and our loved ones devastation, destruction, and more letdowns then we care to admit. We could barely breathe because we thought the end was coming near. Then, one day, we noticed something different about our attitude of being sick and tired. Maybe we are not aware we cried out to God for help, but He heard us and He rushed in to save us from ourselves. He helped us discover we are not alone in this world, because there are millions just like us. God took our brokenness and started to mend us. He took our shortcomings and began to remove them. He took our heart and started to fill it with joy. All of this because we finally turned our will over and surrendered to Him. How great is our God that we get to tell the good things He has done for us, while always giving the glory and praise to Him?

Let us pray:
Dear Heavenly Father, thank you for lifting me up and putting me on solid ground, Amen.

Verse 296

"Wisdom will multiply your days and add years to your life. If you become wise, you will be the one to benefit. If you scorn wisdom, you will be the one to suffer." (Proverbs 9:11-12)

Words for thought:

Alcohol is a mental barrier to us who are alcoholics. The ability to grow in a mature manner has been stunted by all our years of drinking. The sin of pride builds our ego so much so that we cannot hear the advice of others or listen to the words of the Holy Spirit. We put up a brave front on the outside, but inside, we are withering in fear. We begin to have resentments and grudges to the people around us and our hearts become hardened. We tend to hold onto the hurts of our past as if we are punishing the other person. Fellow members, we must heed to the warning in the Big Book that "resentment is the number one offender" (p.64). It's like taking poison and wishing the other person would die. So when we discover God has saved us from ourselves and forgives us our sins, He is also saying we are to forgive others just the same. A part of our recovery is "cleaning up our side of the street" and when that time comes, we will have built enough faith in God to know He will give us the courage to offer our amends. We will no longer have the need to hide, run, or blame, for we will know God's peace.

Let us pray:
Dear Heavenly Father, thank you, because through you, mighty things will happen in my life, Amen.

Verse 297

"The heart of the godly thinks carefully before speaking; the mouth of the wicked overflows with evil words." (Proverbs 15:28)

Words for thought:

For so long in our drinking career, we were unable to react maturely to any situation. Our thoughts rushed out of our mouth without us thinking how they would affect the other person. We lived in our own selfish and self-centered ways, and if we were not happy, our words became explosive, and this only caused us to drink more. The more we drank, the more hostile our words became. Then, one day we accepted God into our heart; this is how we became mature believers in His Word. We started to get out of self and speak well to and of others. See, we don't have to be controlled by every thought that comes to mind; we can display restraint of tongue. Scripture tells us "a kind word is like honey: sweet to the soul and healthy to the body" (Psalm 16:24). So, if we continually stay sober and keep our thoughts on the Lord, then what comes out of our mouth will be pleasing to Him.

Let us pray:
Dear Heavenly Father, thank you for helping me put away my childish speech and desires, Amen.

Verse 298

"But God's truth stands firm like a foundation stone with this inscription: The Lord knows those who are His, and all who belong to the Lord must turn away from evil." (2 Timothy 2:19)

Words for thought:

Our alcoholic behavior kept us away from God, as far away as the east is from the west. It was hard for us to feel any closeness to Him because of our sinful alcoholic desires. We opened the door to Satan and allowed him all the control. We felt guilt and self-loathing and we were lost and afraid. Our egos had to be completely deflated before we could hear God's wisdom, but once we called out to Him, we could feel He was near, and His Word in Psalm 145:18-19 builds us with confidence, because it confirms the "Lord is close to all who call on Him, yes, to all who call on Him in truth. He grants the desires of those who fear Him; He hears their cries for help and rescues them."

Let us pray:
Dear Heavenly Father, thank you for allowing me the privilege to just call upon your name, Amen.

Verse 299

"And it is impossible to please God without faith. Anyone who wants to come to Him must believe that God exists and that He rewards those who sincerely seek Him." (Hebrews 11:6)

Words for thought:

Some alcoholics who are sick and suffering choose not to seek the Kingdom of God. For many of us, we do not deny we've been touched by the right hand of God. Our first spiritual experience came in the way of defeat. Defeat that we can no longer suffer in the disease of alcoholism. Our program is a spiritual one that suggests we find a power greater than ourselves. Our book tells us, "it is easy to let up on the spiritual program of action and rest on our own laurels. We are headed for trouble if we do, for alcohol is a subtle foe" (p.85). At some point in recovery, we must take responsibility for all our actions. When we do this, we cannot deny the transformation that God has brought about in our lives and the lives of our family. So let's look for the moments in our day when the Lord gives us opportunity to love and serve one another.

Let us pray:
Dear Heavenly Father, thank you that by me, believing in you, I am no longer spiritually bankrupt, Amen.

Verse 300

*Let all that I am praise the Lord; with all my heart,
I will praise His holy name. Let all that I am praise
the Lord; may I never forget the good things He does
for me. He forgives my sins and heals my diseases.
He redeems me from death and crowns me with love
and tender mercies. He fills my life with good things.
My youth is renewed like the eagle's. (Psalm 103:1-5)*

Words for thought:

D ealing with alcoholism is a life and death matter. Those of us who are fortunate enough to not live in the denial of our disease lead productive lives. We learn to give all the glory and honor to God because He saved us from our disgrace. In the face of our worst tragedies, God brought us healing. He gave us a spirit of forgiveness, love, and truth. Life is magnificent, even on our worst days, now that we live in the gift of sobriety. We no longer struggle with our day-to-day life and all the decisions we face, simply because we have learned the importance of living in the day!

Let us pray:
Dear Heavenly Father, thank you for the peace you have brought to my life, Amen.

Verse 301

*"Those who follow the right path fear the Lord;
those who take the wrong path despise Him."
(Proverbs 14:2)*

Words for thought:

The idea of never having another drink for the rest of our lives causes us great anxiety. The grief of losing our bottle is like grieving the loss of a beloved friend. Saying goodbye to alcohol can cause deep mental anguish and that is why we, who suffer, are offered a program of recovery to learn how to live just one day at a time: sober. Through this rediscovery process, we will cry on some days and laugh on others, but the great fact remains that we do not have to do it alone, for God is with us. His Word promises even when we walk through the darkest valley, we will not be afraid, for God is close beside us. His rod and His staff will protect and comfort us (Psalm 23:4). So for every day that passes, we need to have the discipline to listen for God's directions in everything we do.

Let us pray:
Dear Heavenly Father, thank you for carrying me through the darkness until I could see the light, Amen.

Verse 302

"You have no obligation to do what your sinful nature urges you to do. For if you live by its dictates, you will die. But if through the power of the Spirit you put to death the deeds of your sinful nature, you will live. For all who are led by the Spirit of God are children of God." (Romans 8:12-14)

Words for thought:

Alcohol took us down a winding and destructive path. It allowed us to become liars, adulterers, thieves, and immature children in our adult bodies. We had become rebellious people who refused to take guidance. Our drunken attitudes were ignited by negative thoughts and offensive speech; our moods were foul and sometimes violent. Our drinking was out of our control and we needed divine intervention. God, who knows all, sees all, and hears all, came to us in a spiritual awakening. We must believe this is a great honor and privilege to be chosen, hand-picked if you will, by God, because not all of us are saved. Remember, He has given us free will to accept this interception, and those of us who are willing to surrender will experience a life-altering change. God is able to turn anyone or anything around for His glory, and for that, we do not take credit. God expects us to be obedient to His Word, regardless of our comfort level while remembering that He has this so we can rest in His power.

Let us pray:

Dear Heavenly Father, thank you for intervening on my behalf when Satan had me living in hell on Earth, Amen.

Verse 303

"But blessed are those who trust in the Lord and have made the Lord their hope and confidence." (Jeremiah 17:7)

Words for thought:

Praying, meditating, and listening to God should be first on our list as our day breaks. This is something we felt we were not deserving of in our old life. Our life of booze caused us agony, sadness, and it kept us from communing with God. Make no mistake about it: in the beginning drinking was fun, we all laughed and had a magical time, but there came a day that we crossed a line, and had to use that bottle to self-medicate. Before we realized it, years went by and so did life, then we discovered we were full-blown alcoholics who could not put the drink down. Even if we did control it for a day or two, in the end, we couldn't stop. This, my friends, is good news because God offers us a program of recovery for healing and self-discovery. This is how we begin to commune with God, because He is full of mercy and grace for us, His children, so He created a miracle in our lives. We are not to just listen to His Words; we must do what they say. Otherwise, we will only be fooling ourselves (James 1:22).

Let us pray:
Dear Heavenly Father, thank you for your gift of salvation, Amen.

Verse 304

"Praise the Lord, for the Lord is good; celebrate His lovely name with music." (Psalm 135:3)

Words for thought:

How many of us cried out in our drunken stupor for our life to just be over, because we couldn't live one more day in this prison of alcoholism? Most of us were unaware of a solution that would lead us to a second lifetime with God as our Savior. We felt doomed and trapped in the gates of hell, until the day we were led by a spiritual awakening. See, God supplied us clarity and then surrounded us with people who understood our malady, the people who came before us, and they explained to us that we had an allergy to alcohol. It finally all made sense to us. The pieces of the puzzle suddenly all started to come together. Then we discovered in God's Word to trust in Him with all our heart and not to depend on our own understanding. It tells us to seek His will in all we do, so He can show us which path to take (Proverbs 3:5-6). Our God is an awesome God who reigns over all the earth. Hallelujah!

Let us pray:
Dear Heavenly Father, thank you for shedding light on my alcoholism, Amen.

Verse 305

"Joyful are people of integrity, who follow the instructions of the Lord." (Psalm 119:1)

Words for thought:

How blessed are we that God saved us from an alcoholic death? We do not have to second-guess this miracle; it simply is. See, God did for us what we could not do for ourselves. Let us move forward and live only for the day, because that is all we have. In fact, the Word tells us, "This is the day the Lord has made. We will rejoice and be glad in it" (Psalm 118:24). The future is not promised to any of us. It is said we only have a daily reprieve from our alcoholism. God will direct us, but sometimes we may be confused to know if the instructions we receive are from God or Satan, so in this case, we pause and remember God doesn't contradict Himself, but Satan does. God's words are never changing, but Satan's words are forever changing. If we feel harmony, we are to move forward in peace, but if there is a seedling of doubt, we pause and question from whom the solution is coming. We can do this with step eleven. This step tells us to seek through prayer and meditation to improve our conscious contact with God and to pray only for the knowledge of His will for us and the power to carry that out. So, in practicing this step daily, we get closer and closer to God, and we will receive the wisdom to know the difference.

Let us pray:
Dear Heavenly Father, thank you for the knowledge that your words are all knowing and all powerful, Amen.

Verse 306

"O Lord, I have longed for your rescue, and your instructions are my delight." (Psalm 119:174)

Words for thought:

How blessed are we who suffer from a disease of alcoholism that we are offered a program of recovery! We are promised by one hundred men and women who have come before us that we have a remedy for our drinking. Once we clear our thinking and look back on how we got sober, we find the suggestions are quite simple in nature. It is by our own desire if we want to go defiantly, kicking and screaming, or putting up our hands in total defeat and surrender. It is instrumental to our soundness of mind that we listen to the good judgment of others when they say "do not drink, go to meetings, believe in God, clean house, and help another alcoholic." Blessed are us who come to God, because He gives us complete renewal of the heart.

Let us pray:
Dear Heavenly Father, thank you that I no longer have to be chained to my disease, Amen.

Verse 307

"Now you are free from your slavery to sin, and you have become slaves to righteous living."
(Romans 6:18)

Words for thought:

While sick and suffering from our disease, our minds were in constant chatter. We continuously tried to manipulate and control every situation with every person, place, and thing; we wanted things our way. We became so consumed with our alcoholic behavior that our passage to God was blocked. We couldn't feel His presence, nor hear His promptings. We were so caught up in bondage of self that we would rather be dead then spend another day drunk. Then, one day, in our weakest moment, God's prompting was louder than Satan's whisper; the Lord said, "take up the shield of faith, with which you can extinguish all the flaming arrows of the evil one" (Ephesians 6:16). It was at this point, this split second, that our footing became stronger, and we were able to reach out for help and thus begin our journey to God and recovery.

Let us pray:
Dear Heavenly Father, thank you for quieting my mind long enough for me to hear your voice, Amen.

Verse 308

*"So rejoice in the Lord and be glad all you who obey
Him! Shout for joy, all you whose hearts are pure!"
(Psalm 32:11)*

Words for thought:

While we drowned our sorrows in the bottle, God paved a road to recovery for us. He continually helped us along the path to freedom until we reached sobriety. He put us on higher ground so we may follow His commandments, keep faith in His Word, and help others along the road to the same destiny. The result of putting the drink down is that it made us brand-new. We are made into something different, someone better than before. We are not to fool ourselves, however, into thinking this is going to be a free ride. There will be many struggles ahead, but God will intervene on our behalf when we remain loyal to Him. So ask yourself today if your heart is where it needs to be, because it is only when our heart is right that God can continue its renewal.

Let us pray:
Dear Heavenly Father, thank you for giving us a new life to live peacefully one day at a time, Amen.

Verse 309

"I will praise the Lord at all times. I will constantly speak His praises." (Psalm 34:1)

Words for thought:

We are to lay down our alcoholic burdens, hurts, struggles, and fears right at the feet of God. He knows we are broken, so we need not come to Him in shame. He wants us to come to Him exactly as we are, then He can build us up in His love and forgiveness. God wants us to humbly walk down the narrow path He has already created for us and once we surrender our heart to Him, He is able to bring us healing, courage, and strength. He will give us the wisdom to know the difference. Philippians 4:8-9 leaves us with these words:

Fix your thoughts on what is true, and honorable, and right, and pure, and lovely, and admirable. Think about things that are excellent and worthy of praise. Keep putting into practice all you learned and received from me, everything you heard from me and saw me doing. Then the God of peace will be with you.

Let us pray:
Dear Heavenly Father, thank you for filling my life with the Holy Spirit, Amen.

Verse 310

"Humble yourselves before the Lord, and He will lift you up in honor." (James 4:10)

Words for thought:

In the hands of God, we are strong. If we are firmly anchored in His Word, then evil cannot drag us into sin. We need to follow His commands, obey His words, and His blessings will overflow into our lives. We must avoid any distraction with which Satan baits us. He wants us to cheat, lie, steal, and drink. He is a liar, but not our God. Our Lord cares about us in every situation and He will provide what we need at just the right time.

Let us pray:
Dear Heavenly Father, thank you for your guidance that led me to help someone today. All I had to do was get out of self by going to a meeting and sharing with another alcoholic, Amen.

Verse 311

"You can enter God's kingdom only through the narrow gate. The highway to Hell is broad, and its gate is wide for the many who choose that way." (Matthew 7:13)

Words for thought:

The Big Book is a guide that aids us in getting better. In the fifth chapter of "How it Works" is a sentence that reads: "rarely have we seen a person fail who has thoroughly followed our path" (p. 59-60). This is coming from the first one hundred men and women who attempted to live a sober life. They displayed great success in not drinking one day at a time, and over eighty years later, it still works, if we work at it. So, we have to ask ourselves honestly, "Can this work for me too?" Yes, when we remain open and willing to follow their guidance. Let's look at some key sentences from this chapter:

- "completely give themselves to this simple program"
- "have rigorous honesty"
- "we beg of you to be fearless and thorough from the very beginning"
- "let go absolutely or the result is nil"
- "remember we deal with alcohol-cunning, baffling, powerful"
- "but there is one who has all power that one is God may you find Him now"
- "willing to grow along spiritual lines"
- "spiritual progress, not spiritual perfection."

They outlined steps that if we take action on, then our success rate will rise to victory. However, we must remain humble, because alcohol is a subtle enemy that attacks through every emotion we feel, and folks, it does not discriminate. Remember this: we are on a journey without a destination, so we stay away from thoughts such as "we've got this," or "I don't need a meeting," or even. "I don't have time for God this morning," these are traps. We are never to get comfortable and rest on our own laurels in sobriety, for when we do, relapse is a guarantee.

Let us pray:
Dear Heavenly Father, thank you for giving us your word in Scripture as a way of life, Amen.

Verse 312

*"I pray that God, the source of hope, will fill you com-
pletely with joy and peace because you trust in Him.
Then you will overflow with confident hope through
the power of the Holy Spirit." (Romans 15:13)*

Words for thought:

Isn't it awesome that through our alcoholism, we have been
offered a gift of sobriety by the hand of God? We had to put
away old ideas and prejudices against the Almighty and bow
to Him with gratitude and belief. We had to put the drink down
long enough for our thinking to catch up to what is truly in our
hearts. When we open our heart to God, He gives us hope, joy,
and love. With Him, we discover we are not inferior to anyone,
but everyone, in God's eyes, are His children, and we are wonderfully made. It just so happened that because of our disease,
we took the long and winding road to Him, but in the end, we
finally came to a place of rest, peace, and renewal of heart.

Let us pray:
*Dear Heavenly Father, thank you that it doesn't matter how I
came to you, but that you accept me as I am, Amen.*

Verse 313

"And we know that in all things God works for the good of those who love Him, who have been called according to His purpose." (Romans 8:28)

Words for thought:

Satan is a liar. John 10:10 tells us His purpose is to steal, kill, and destroy. He pulls us downward to destruction and a loss of hope. We must refuse to allow him to discourage us. For every temptation, every evil, every lie, every promise that Satan proposes, Jesus taught us to say, "Get behind me, Satan." Every fear, every sin, and every delusion was made up from our own alcoholism, but when we continuously pray on purpose to God and keep faith daily, He then works all things for good! God opened a door for us; a way out. He, God, and recovery are so much more powerful than our disease! As long as we build a solid foundation on all things good, we will then enter into a brand-new way of life. A life built beyond our wildest dreams!

Let us pray:
Dear Heavenly Father, thank you for guiding me to enjoy my life to its fullest, Amen.

Verse 314

"The righteous cry out, and the lord hears them; He delivers them from all their troubles. The Lord is close to the brokenhearted and saves those who are crushed in spirit." (Psalm 34:17-18)

Words for thought:

Isn't it awesome that God gives us His forgiveness and offers us serenity for all our drunkenness? We must learn that we cannot handle our alcoholism alone. Old feelings and wants will creep into our mindset, so we are to stay vigilant in our walk with the Almighty. We are not beyond forgiveness and we are not worse than everybody else. In fact, we need God and another human being. We must remember that isolation breeds deceitfulness. God has given us a spiritual gift to help ourselves and each other. Let's do so without hesitation, because a part of our sobriety will depend on it.

Let us pray:
Dear Heavenly Father, thank you for being with me this day, Amen.

Verse 315

"Don't let evil conquer you, but conquer evil by doing good." (Romans 12:21)

Words for thought:

Scripture in Psalm 46:10 reads: "Be still and know that I am God." One day at some point in our disease, we had our spiritual awakening. For some, this experience was a white light. The kind that our cofounder experienced. While others were significant, but subtle in nature. However the case, we all knew we couldn't continue life the way we were—drunk. We had an inkling there might be something better than just death. So when the day came that God called upon us, we heard Him. See, we are the blessed ones. We are called to a higher purpose other than to just waste away. God promises to be our shield, our protector, our defender, our guide, and our everlasting rock. Do we want to go back to the gates of Hell?

Let us pray:
Dear Heavenly Father, thank you for bringing me into your presence and keeping me safe, Amen.

Verse 316

"There are six things the Lord hates, no, seven things He detests: Haughty eyes, a lying tongue, hands that kill the innocent, a heart that plots evil, feet that race to do wrong, a false witness who pours out lies, a person who sows discord in a family." (Proverbs 6:16-19)

Words for thought:

We were so caught up in self that we didn't see the destruction our alcoholism was leaving behind. We went on merrily with our drinking, acting as if it was the solution to all our problems. For many years, we convinced ourselves that we were not heading for catastrophe. In fact, we were the last to know we needed an intervention. Although, in the end, we could no longer deny the bumps, bruises, cuts, and ill health. What can wipe away our sins? How can we receive forgiveness of all our transgressions? How can we *not* take a drink today? We do not drink today because of God. He tells us to have faith and believe He, not we, will increase our confidence by associating with people of the same malady. He will wipe our sins clean. We will learn from those around us in program, and when we listen, we will find out how they learned to stay sober, just one day at a time.

Let us pray:
Dear Heavenly Father, thank you for shedding light on my tunnel of darkness, Amen.

Verse 317

"So let us come boldly to the throne of our gra-
cious God. There we will receive His mercy, and
we will find grace to help us when we need it most."
(Hebrews 4:16)

Words for thought:

U pon entering a program of recovery, we quickly learn God can and will remove our obsession and compulsion for alcohol. He will freely give us His grace, even when we are not deserving of it. God's grace does not hold onto our disappointments, anger, or pain—His grace forgives our sins. Every morning, every night, and every moment in between, we give our shortcomings to Him and He absolves our faults and failures. God knows our heart, and when we repent, His love rains upon us.

Let us pray:
Dear Heavenly Father, thank you for knowing what I need,
before I even come to you in prayer, Amen.

Verse 318

"Dear brothers and sisters, I close my letter with these last words: Be joyful. Grow to maturity. Encourage each other. Live in harmony and peace. Then the God of love and peace will be with you." (2 Corinthians 13:11)

Words for thought:

We asked God to show us the path to walk and He walked along with us. We asked Him for the words to speak from our mouth, so we may speak them to others. We have come to Him shattered by our alcoholism and we begged Him to have mercy on us. Then, one day at a time, God helped us rebuild our house. We began with His spiritual arch and then, brick by brick, slowly and steadily, we began to stand upright again and take our place back in this world. God never judges us, He never gives up on us, and most importantly, God will never leave us alone. His words are simple and His grace is abundant. He gives us courage to be fair and honest with ourselves, and with each other, in all we do. He expects us to show authentic love, compassion, and mercy to our fellowman. We will walk humbly before God, thinking less of ourselves, while aligning our will with His. Hallelujah!

Let us pray:
Dear Heavenly Father, thank you for everything, because everything I have comes from you, Amen.

Verse 319

"I listen carefully to what God the Lord is saying, for He speaks peace to His faithful people. But let them not return to their foolish ways." (Psalm 85:8)

Words for thought:

In our disease, within our minds, we began to hate everything about being alive. Our hearts were stirred up with resentments, revenge, annoyance, and indignation. We began to isolate against family and friends because we felt their judgment against our drinking. We were completely and utterly driven by our alcoholism. We felt we were going to die with the bottle in hand, but we also found we could not survive without it. Our perspective on life was blurry at best, until we learned that abstinence from "all" alcohol was the key to success. We had to say goodbye to "John Barleycorn" once and for all, if we were to regain our dignity and self-worth. In sobriety, overtime, amazing things happen. God entered our life and we found serenity. We found soundness of mind, and in this Scripture, we received this promise: "I am leaving you with a gift: peace of mind and heart. And the peace I give is a gift the world cannot give. So don't be troubled or afraid" (John 14:27).

Let us pray:
Dear Heavenly Father, thank you for saving me from a death of alcoholic agony, Amen.

Verse 320

"Let my soul be at rest again, for the Lord has been good to me." (Psalm 116:7)

Words for thought:

We should not always trust our feelings simply because they are fickle. Our soul begins feeling irritable, restless, and discontent. While drinking, our emotions were tumultuous. We were incapable of controlling them when fueled with alcohol. Once we overcame the obsession to be drunk, we began to lean on God for all things, including the management of our emotions. Will life overwhelm us at times so much so that we want to drink? Yes, but on our journey with God and the twelve steps, we have discovered we have grown in His Word and "no matter what," we do not have to drink.

Let us pray:
Dear Heavenly Father, thank you for giving me fellow believers so I am not all alone, Amen.

Verse 321

"If you listen to constructive criticism, you will be at home among the wise." (Proverbs 15:31)

Words for thought:

The important question to ask ourselves upon awakening is if God is our closest friend. He created a miracle for us when He brought us into a fellowship of sobriety. He knew we were not alone in our walk with Satan, so He gave us one another. He said, "Go and share your experience, strength, and hope to the next suffering alcoholic." God does not want us to regret our past, but He wants us to learn from it, and have the wisdom to make our decisions based on what will make us happy later. We suffered far too long with frustration, ego, anxiety, and resentments. We were unloving, harsh, and angry. We lashed out at those who loved us the most, because we were too drunk to rationalize right from wrong. Ecclesiastes 7:9 tells us to "control our temper, for an anger labels us a fool," but we just could not stop. Our self-will was powerful and we let Satan rule our decisions until that one day when God saved our life. That one undeniable moment of clarity that only God could give. So let us ask again, "Is God my closest friend?"

Let us pray:
Dear Heavenly Father, thank you for your wisdom that I will need today, tomorrow, and forever, Amen.

Verse 322

"I will bless the Lord who guides me; even at night my heart instructs me. I know the Lord is always with me. I will not be shaken, for He is right beside me." (Psalm 16:7-8)

Words for thought:

We were convinced if we drank enough alcohol, it would drown out the chaos in our minds. It was like being on a merry-go-round, spinning and spinning. The only time we had rest is when we blacked out or passed out. We knew we couldn't live life this way any longer. We were sick and we were tired of the insanity of doing the same thing over and over again. God did not put us on this earth to suffer; His proof is in Jeremiah 29:11 when He tells us, "'For I know the plans I have for you,' says the Lord. 'They are plans for good and not for disaster, to give you a future and a hope.'" We are not to handle our difficult situations, happy situations, or any celebrations as drunkards. We are to handle them as God's children, observing His commands, embracing His words, saying, "My God, I will take joy in doing your will, for your instructions are written on my heart" (Psalm 40:8).

Let us pray:

Dear Heavenly Father, thank you for calming the storm that invades my mind day and night, Amen.

Verse 323

"Don't worry about anything; instead, pray about everything. Tell God what you need, and thank Him for all he has done. Then you will experience God's peace, which exceeds anything we can understand. His peace will guard your hearts and minds as you live in Christ Jesus." (Philippians 4:6-7)

Words for thought:

Sometimes we thought our lives were doomed forever because we were alcoholics. Yet, God was working something out for us which was much greater than our plan. Many of us came crawling on hand and knee for a miracle, and because God loves us so much, He gave us that miracle, but now there is work to do. God also supplies us with life-changing instructions to heed when we are willing to trust His Word. His Word tells us we should get all the advice and instruction we can, so we will be wise for the rest of our life (Proverbs 19:20). What is important for us is to accept not all of our challenges will be pleasant or easy, but we can rest knowing that through our faith in God, we will never have to drink again.

Let us pray:
Dear Heavenly Father, thank you for the joy you have given me, Amen.

Verse 324

"Keep me safe, O God, for I have come to you for refuge." (Psalm 16:1)

Words for thought:

So many of us suffered many, many years with our alcoholism. We suffered from a magnitude of guilt, shame, and remorse. Our motives were corrupted by our own selfish and self-centered desires so we settled for living in the snares of Satan instead of the riches of Christ Jesus. We were lost in the wilderness and chose to live by sight rather than by faith. However, somewhere along our path, we decided we could no longer live in our drunken misery, and God heard our plea and gave us a glimpse of hope. We cannot explain it, but we felt a sudden calm, a new desire to want to get well. We began to believe and have faith that God will empower us with inner strength and that He will lead us to victory over our disease. Hallelujah!

Let us pray:
Dear Heavenly Father, thank you for saving me from further pain and sorrow, Amen.

Verse 325

"All praise to God, the Father of our Lord Jesus Christ. God is our merciful Father and the source of all comfort. He comforts us in all our troubles so that we can comfort others. When they are troubled, we will be able to give them the same comfort God has given us." (2 Corinthians 1:3-4)

Words for thought:

A fact remains for us admitted alcoholics, that we are only "one drink away from being drunk." We, in the program, cannot afford the luxury of complacency. We must be willing to initiate the twelve steps into our daily life, all day, every day. When we read God's Word, it reinforces us to not only look out for our own interests, but to take an interest in others too (Philippians 2:4). In sobriety, we cannot keep what we have been given, and so it is with God's Word we must share the good news among our fellow members. Time after time, we will see God's many blessings in our life and we can be at peace knowing His light will guide us through and keep us safe. God has given us victory, but are we working our program to the best of our ability? Are we sharing with another alcoholic? Or are we allowing our foundation to fracture?

Let us pray:
Dear Heavenly Father, thank you for giving me the ability to stand on my own, sober, Amen.

Verse 326

*"People with integrity walk safely, but those who follow
crooked paths will be exposed." (Proverbs 10:9)*

Words for thought:

Every day that we awakened, our attitude was that of needing
a drink. For years and years, we could not accept our persons,
places, and things as they were, so we drank ourselves into a
life of complete denial. We thought this was the easier arrange-
ment to hide behind, so we did not have to face reality. Yet, there
came a point when our alcohol no longer fixed what was broken
inside us. We could no longer ignore the wrong path on which
we traveled. We began to learn we could no longer live worldly
and we needed a spiritual change on this earth. We needed to
set right what was wrong with us and invite God into our lives.
We needed to fix our attitude and we needed to become willing
to change.

Let us pray:
*Dear Heavenly Father, thank you for showing me mercy during
my times of trouble, Amen.*

Verse 327

"Open my eyes to see the wonderful truths in your instructions." (Psalm 119:18)

Words for thought:

The only thing that many of us drunks suffer from is the inability to accept our powerlessness. We tried many methods to prove that we could drink like normal people, and each time, we failed miserably. Let's face it: we loved the effect that alcohol had on us. One drink was never enough and then two drinks, and three and four, and before we knew it, we woke with the remorse of not knowing what we did or didn't do. It is important for us to know we reap what we sow, and if we are always pleasing the flesh, then only destruction can occur. If we turn our ways to the Lord, great things will begin to happen. He can deliver us hope and prosperity; He will take care of us and give us peace. God loves us unconditionally, and He is waiting for us, so let us with sober minds be ready to receive the Lord's many blessings that He will bestow upon us and our families.

Let us pray:

Dear Heavenly Father, thank you for not letting my drunken beginning, become my fatal end, Amen.

Verse 328

"If I were you I would go to God and present my case to Him. He does great things too marvelous to understand. He performs countless miracles." (Job 5:8-9)

Words for thought:

We sought relief in the bottom of a bottle. All God could do was wait—wait for us to surrender our control, will, and way of life to Him. We could not see it because we were blinded by our alcoholism, and we couldn't hear Him because we lived in Satan's den. Yet, when our fight was over, we realized God's hands held us tight the whole time. See, there are no coincidences in God's world; only miracles. Although we cannot win the war of our alcoholism, what we can do is learn to fight the fight and live with our disease one day at a time. We are to release the power our alcoholism has on us and want what the Lord wants for us: love, joy, peace, patience, kindness, goodness, gentleness, faithfulness and self-control (Galatians 5:22-23). So are we ready to trust Him in all our affairs?

Let us pray:
Dear Heavenly Father, thank you for opening my eyes to your many miracles, Amen.

Verse 329

*"For the world offers only a craving for physical plea-
sure, a craving for everything we see, and pride in our
achievements and possessions. These are not from
our Father, but are from this world." (1 John 2:16)*

Words for thought:

We all have had regret. We all have experienced some kind of indiscretion. We all have suffered sorrow and despair, and for many, these things consumed our life. So what choice did we make? We hid behind the bottle. We gave up in defeat. We pushed family and friends away until we were all alone, drowning in our own self-pity. We avoided looking in the mirror until the one day we finally saw ourselves looking back. The sight we saw was frightening and disturbing. Our reflection was a woeful image of what we had become. Somehow that heart-rending stare back at us spoke, and we knew we needed saving. We were completely stripped of our dignity, but God offered us a way; a way back to life. A way for us to enter onto a spiritual journey of recovery. Make no mistake: it is a pathway of gut-wrenching work. So, the question is, are we open, willing, and honest enough to go down that path of sobriety? God is waiting and He tells us "lazy people want much but get little, but those who work hard will prosper" (Proverbs 13:4).

Let us pray:
*Dear Heavenly Father, thank you for giving me a bridge to come
back to a life worth living, Amen.*

Verse 330

"God blesses those who work for peace, for they will be called the children of God." (Matthew 5:9)

Words for thought:

At the end of our drinking career, we were spiritually bankrupt. We were isolated from the world and for many of us we felt like we had nothing to offer family, let alone society. There was that final day for all of us that we could no longer carry the burden of our alcoholism, and all the insanity that came with it. Something began to tell us that there was more to life than living it as a drunk. Within this thinking, we somehow allowed God to make His voice be heard and we had our first spiritual awakening. We suddenly realized there was a "higher state" for living. We became acutely aware we were doing the same thing over and over expecting different results. So we gave sobriety a chance, and one day at a time, our minds became serene, our hands no longer shook, our eyes were brighter, and we turned our will over to the care of God.

Let us pray:
Dear Heavenly Father, thank you for bringing me back from the gates of hell, Amen.

Verse 331

"Do everything without complaining and arguing, so that no one can criticize you. Live clean, innocent lives as children of God, shining like bright lights in a world full of crooked and perverse people."
(Philippians 2:14-15)

Words for thought:

Let us not get caught up in self-indulgence. Our drinking behaviors of being a liar, cheat, and thief are over. That is not saying we will be perfect, because we lived with our defects for many years, but the point is, we now have a guide to staying sober. The twelve steps to our program is a gift and we must strive day by day to be better people. Now that we are of sober mind, our wounds can begin to heal. We are able to take a look at ourselves and know that we do not want to go back to old behaviors of insanity. We now know when we feel overwhelmed or confused that we are to go to God in prayer and meditate on His Word, because His promises are abundant. Let's take a look at what Isaiah 40:29-33 says about His promises:

He gives power to the weak and strength to the powerless. Even youths will become weak and tired, and young men will fall in exhaustion. But those who trust in the Lord will find new strength. They will soar high on wings like eagles. They will run and not grow weary. They will walk and not faint.

Let us pray:
Dear Heavenly Father, thank you for healing my brokenness, Amen.

Verse 332

"Look straight ahead, and fix your eyes on what lies
before you. Mark out a straight path for your feet;
stay on the safe path. Don't get sidetracked; keep
your feet from following evil." (Proverbs 4:25-27)

Words for thought:

One of our greatest challenges in sobriety is self-will. The alcoholic, meaning us, are, for the most part, prideful, egotistical, grandiose, argumentative, lazy, and impatient. We were not even aware of all these shortcomings due to our inability to get better. Yet, the beautiful thing about self-will is that it can be disciplined. All we have to do is say no to the drink and yes to God. He awaits our surrender and He forgives us our sins. Simple, right? Yes, because you trust God or you do not; we choose. When we choose God, we will live a life full of freedom and happiness. So let us allow our love and dependence on Christ be a witness for all to see.

Let us pray:
Dear Heavenly Father, thank you for loving me, Amen.

Verse 333

"The godly are directed by honesty; the wicked fall beneath their load of sin." (Proverbs 11:5)

Words for thought:

Thy will, not mine, be done! The question is: what is the will of God for ourselves? It is obedience to His commands. Once we open that door to Him, we will know in our hearts what is morally right, because it is known in God's Word that He does not listen to sinners, but He is ready to hear those who worship Him and do His will (John 9:31). See, God wants to empower us, but only if we surrender to His glorious truths. He wants us to have an intimate relationship with Him, if we believe. He wants us to have gratitude in all He does, so we can appreciate His love for us. When we become of sober mind, we will want to tell others the good news. So are you ready for the will of God?

Let us pray:
Dear Heavenly Father, thank you for filling my life with serenity, Amen.

Verse 334

"Those who know your name trust in you, for you,
O Lord, do not abandon those who search for you."
(Psalm 9:10)

Words for thought:

S ometimes, in our program, we start to get comfortable. This could take as little as thirty days or as long as thirty years. We have heard many times in the rooms that meetings are our "medicine," so why would we stop going? After all, wouldn't a diabetic be the fool if they suddenly stopped their medication? They know they will die. Well, so would we who suffer the disease of alcoholism. Speaking from experience, it doesn't take long for our character defects to rear their ugly heads once we quit our "medicine." We then convince ourselves we know better than God, and soon after that, a drink doesn't sound so bad. As a matter of fact, we become the drunks we once were. So we ask ourselves, "Am I being diligent with my program or am I beginning to rest on my own laurels?"

Let us pray:
Dear Heavenly Father, thank you for helping me continue my journey one day at a time, Amen.

Verse 335

"The Lord is watching everywhere, keeping His eye on both evil and the good." (Proverbs 15:3)

Words for thought:

All of our blessings flow directly from God. Sometimes we may ask, "How am I supposed to know if it's coming from Him and not Satan?" That is easy, because God does not fill us with confusion. God is perfect love, perfect peace, and perfectly loyal to all His children. When we finally hear and listen after we cried out in distress, "Please release me from my alcoholism," He graciously, mercifully, and compassionately relieved us, if just for today, from our desire to drink. So now it is up to us to decide how we are going to bare this glorious fruit. We are made to cling to God's Word so we can live a happy, joyous, and free life! So let's keep knocking, never giving up while pursuing Him in prayer.

Let us pray:
Dear Heavenly Father, thank you for filling me with you word, Amen.

Verse 336

*"But let us who live in the light be clearheaded, pro-
tected by the armor of faith and love, and wearing
as our helmet the confidence of our salvation." (1
Thessalonians 5:8)*

Words for thought:

After a while in our program, we began to slowly see ourselves as God sees us: beautiful and wonderfully made in His
image. This process took a significant amount of time, because
for years, we convinced ourselves that we were not good to
ourselves nor any good to others. Drinking brought about many
mixed emotions, and we deeply felt inadequate to face life on
life's terms. Yet, sobriety teaches us that it is okay to make mistakes and to say "I am sorry" and make amends. It teaches us
humility, tolerance, and love of others. Eventually, our need to
be alone will diminish and we will want to be part of society
again. Our new-found relationship with the Lord will continuously grow and we will allow Him to lead us to victory.

Let us pray:
*Dear Heavenly Father, thank you for allowing me to grow in
your Word day by day, Amen.*

Verse 337

"Give all your worries and cares to God, for He cares about you." (1 Peter 5:7)

Words for thought:

Our circumstances in life can change in an instant. We look at the twenty-four hours ahead and make our plans, but what happens when our day is disrupted by something that derails us? Do we drink or do we trust God? If we have vowed to believe God in *all* things, then we know He is always with us. In fact, He is right beside us, protecting us, loving us, and sheltering us. Whatever we are dealing with, we must believe God is our strength. Hallelujah!

Let us pray:
Dear Heavenly Father, thank you for being my stronghold in calmness or calamity, Amen.

Verse 338

"Greed brings grief to the whole family, but those who hate bribes will live." (Proverbs 15:27)

Words for thought:

We, who are alcoholics, sit high on indignation. We are judgmental and therefore judge ourselves with a severe tongue. We show no true kindness or love toward family or fellow man. God wants us to identify the obstacle that is in our way, so we are no longer distracted from its evil way. We can no longer live in the denial of our alcoholism, because it keeps us far away from the grace God wants to bestow on us. God is always calling out to us to make change, but are we listening? Do we truly want to move past the pain of our sickness, or do we want to die a suffering death? Let us rest in the Word of God from Proverbs 4:20-22: "My child, pay attention to what I say. Listen carefully to my words. Don't lose sight of them. Let them penetrate deep into your heart, for they bring life to those who find them, and healing to their whole body."

Let us pray,
Dear Heavenly Father, thank you for bringing me back from the darkness, Amen.

Verse 339

"People ruin their lives by their own foolishness and then are angry at the Lord." (Proverbs 19:3)

Words for thought:

We all created some kind of destruction while being intoxicated. We caused great misdeeds against our families, and we did this day after day, promising we would never do it again. The guilt, shame, and remorse that built up in our hearts was overbearing, so we stayed in denial of our sins and we drank to forget. Yet, our salvation is the greatest gift from our Lord, because He said, "Father, forgive them, for they know not what they are doing" (Luke 23:34). God took mercy on our weaknesses and our ignorance, and then He gifted us alcoholics with a program of recovery. He gave us a path, a blueprint, and a fellowship so we can all learn to love again, and He offered us forgiveness so we may forgive ourselves as well as others. So tell me, how great is our Lord!

Let us pray:
Dear Heavenly Father, thank you for giving us your Son, Amen.

Verse 340

> *"Backsliders get what they deserve; good people
> receive their reward." (Proverbs 14:14)*

Words for thought:

We used to be so busy filling our days with alcohol. We kept missing the miracle of God because we chose to live in free will day after day. We barely took into consideration the despair we caused our loved ones. We turned a blind eye to the destruction we left in our path, and the ripple effect didn't stop with us because we so carelessly carried it into the next generation: our children. Once we became willing to do as the Lord says in Matthew 4:17, "Repent of your sins and return to God, for the kingdom of heaven is near," is when we understood step three. We saw that faith began to surround us and our hearts became open to God's Word, and our minds became less troubled from all its demons. Remember, we must not stop there, because God says to carry His message to the next sick and suffering.

Let us pray:
Dear Heavenly Father, thank you that I can now live in your glorious peace, Amen.

Verse 341

"We can make our own plans, but the Lord gives the right answer." (Proverbs 16:1)

Words for thought:

For many years, we chose to follow a pathway toward a lower power at work in our lives. We didn't know we needed discipline from a power greater than ourselves. It was difficult for many of us to cross that river of denial of our alcoholism and come before God. We did not want to take full responsibility for living in the flesh and giving up our deep-rooted desires—the desires that almost killed us. Yet, we questioned: how are we supposed to live, even if it is just for today, without a drink? How do we avoid being swallowed up by our shortcomings that come along with our disease? Well, we do it by trusting God, and praising Him, and by believing in Him, because He has afforded us a beautiful harvest of mercy. Let us make today the day that we do not allow any distractions keep us from God. Let us have faith that He has a new, sober plan for us and for our days to come.

Let us pray:

Dear Heavenly Father, thank you for making my life worth living again, Amen.

Verse 342

"The Lord says, 'I will rescue those who love me. I will protect those who trust in my name. When they call on me, I will answer; I will be with them in trouble. I will rescue and honor them. I will reward them with long life and give them my salvation.'" (Psalm 91:14-16)

Words for thought:

During our drunken days, we couldn't imagine putting others' best interests ahead of our drinking. We were selfish, self-absorbed, and completely intolerant of anyone who did not drink as we did. We ignored godly correction over and over again and sometimes led others down the wrong path. It wasn't until we let God in and humbled ourselves that we could see our life the way that it was: sick, broken, and tattered. Yet, God gave us a new lighted path to change our journey. He told us to come follow Him and live by His Word and to bring others along with us. Let us simply live our lives according to His purpose, while remaining grateful for His mercy.

Let us pray:

Dear Heavenly Father, thank you for being my stronghold and refuge, Amen.

Verse 343

"How sweet your words taste to me; they are sweeter than honey. Your commandments give me under-standing; no wonder I hate every false way of life. Your word is a lamp to guide my feet and a light for my path." (Psalm 119:103-105)

Words for thought:

God allows us spiritual experiences at different times in our sobriety. As long as we remain sober we can expect small gifts of miracles along the way. All we need to do is have the virtue of being patient. See, God is watching us and He pays special attention to how we are walking and behaving through our trials and tribulations in life. Are we kind, tolerant, compassionate, and loving, or are we worrisome, anxious, and disobedient? We need to be sincerely worshipping God throughout our day, every day, with our whole hearts, because He saved us. He took us from the stormy waters and placed us high on level ground so we may build our foundation on Him, not our alcoholism.

Let us pray:
Dear Heavenly Father, thank you for your lovingkindness and saving me with your truth, Amen.

Verse 344

"No discipline is enjoyable while it is happening-it's painful! But afterward there will be a peaceful harvest of right living for those who are trained in this way." (Hebrews 12:11)

Words for thought:

The day we turn our will and lives over to the care of God, miracles begin to happen. The first miracle we receive is the gift of never having to put another drink to our perched lips again. All the self-loathing, all its misery, and all the chaos it created in our mind finally comes to rest. We begin to fill our lives with the knowledge of our program and the love of God. Soon afterward, we are instructed to go out and pay forward what was freely given to us, to our fellow man who still suffers. We can do this, we can believe in His Word, and we can obey them. We can confess our sins to God and all will be wiped clean, for the Lord has declared, "I am the way, the truth, and the life. No one can come to the Father except through me." Hallelujah, we've been saved!

Let us pray:
Dear Heavenly Father, thank you for giving me your truth so I may sing it joyfully to the world, Amen.

Verse 345

"And I am convinced that nothing can ever separate us from God's love. Neither death nor life, neither angels nor demons, neither our fears for today nor our worries about tomorrow - not even the powers of hell can separate us from God's love." (Romans 8:38)

Words for thought:

We have held onto so much of the wretchedness of our past. So much so that we eliminated all the good that was in and around us by drinking. This caused us great dislike and resentment toward family, friends, and foes. All of this blocked the love of God from our hearts. It was much easier to pick up the bottle and drown out all the noise. So what we needed was a complete change of heart to live life on God's terms. We needed to put our disease at rest and allow God to redeem our past. We needed to follow His will and allow our hearts to be open to His love and tolerance. Yet, the questions are: will we take that crucial step to forgive and repent? Are we willing to find our way back to God's loving arms? Are we willing to receive His love? It is decision time: yes or no.

Let us pray:
Dear Heavenly Father, thank you for loving me while knowing all of my wrongdoings, Amen.

Verse 346

"Love the Lord your God with all your heart, and with all your soul, and with all your strength." (Deuteronomy 6:5)

Words for thought:

When we pray, we have to ask God for those things that will help us grow. Daily, we ask Him for guidance in love, knowledge, and understanding of others. We pray for acceptance because it truly is the key to life. Throughout our day, we are to look for moments that gives us an opportunity to do good for others. Remember, God loves us and cares about our inner beings. Wherever we go, God is with us and our life should reflect the love we have for Him.

Let us pray:
Dear Heavenly Father, thank you for my hope and courage. Thank you for loving me first, Amen.

Verse 347

*"I will exalt you, my God and King, and praise your
name forever and ever. I will praise you every day;
yes, I will praise you forever. Great is the Lord! He
is most worthy of praise! No one can measure His
greatness." (Psalm 145:1-3)*

Words for thought:

Upon awakening, life can seem so daunting. For reasons
unknown, we feel restless, irritable, and discontent. We suffer
from the disease of alcoholism, and we know we cannot pick up
that first drink. In the rooms, we can see those of us who have
been given the gift of sobriety from God. We have been given
a program to learn, not only how to live a sober life, but to face
life without fear. God teaches us how to love again and how to
be kind and have tolerance for persons, places, and things. We
begin to put God first in all we do, as we pray, "O Lord, hear
me as I pray; pay attention to my groaning. Listen to my cry
for help, my King and my God, for I pray to no one but you.
Listen to my voice in the morning, Lord. Each morning I bring
my requests to you and wait expectantly" (Psalm 5:1-3).

Let us pray:
*Dear Heavenly Father, thank you for hearing my voice when I
petition you for courage and strength, Amen.*

Verse 348

"I will praise you, Lord, with all my heart; I will tell of all the marvelous things you have done." (Psalm 9:1)

Words for thought:

Here we sit, completely surrounded by family and friends, yet somehow, we feel distant and alone. We couldn't understand the frowned-upon looks and the pitiful stares that came our way as we drank one drink after another. We didn't comprehend, because we thought we were the life of the party, but unfortunately, we were not the life, we were an embarrassment to our loved ones. So when we were presented with a way to get well, we were skeptical, because nothing else worked, however, we discovered we are not alone, after all. We have an opportunity to escape our alcoholism. God is waiting for us to accept His invitation for healing. With His presence and His Word, God will heal all the brokenness in our hearts. When we feel alone, confused, and caught up in self, we pray. We pray on God's words, and then we offer Him all that we are, and all that we have, and all that we do. Hallelujah!

Let us pray:
Dear Heavenly Father, thank you for going before me and making a path for me to follow, Amen.

Verse 349

"I will praise you, Lord, with all my heart: I will tell of all the marvelous things you have done." (Psalm 9:1)

Words for thought:

Throughout our day, we need to consistently remind ourselves that we have received a gift: the gift of sobriety. After a while, we become grateful and that gratitude becomes our awe-inspiring mantra, because for us alcoholics, ungratefulness is one of our greatest enemies. When our hearts and minds become open and willing, we will give thanks to the Lord, for He is good. We will not look back on our days with regret, but look forward to the future in hope and with thankfulness. We can see the future wide-eyed and hopeful because God has magnificent plans for our lives.

Let us pray:
Dear Heavenly Father, thank you for giving me new hope for my present day, Amen.

Verse 350

"People who conceal their sins will not prosper, but if they confess and turn from them, they will receive mercy." (Proverbs 28:13)

Words for thought:

The power of our Lord is everlasting. He is but one whisper away from saving our soul. Sometimes, we do not feel deserving of His grace, because of the sins committed by our drunken sprees, but He still says to come to Him and repent and we will be redeemed. We are not who we used to be, so once God cleanses our stains, we are set free to do His will; remember, "thy will be done." We are to be painstakingly honest with our regret and acknowledge our sins, because God knows our heart. He sees we are good people with an illness, trying to get better. This is why He created a program of recovery. So let's share God's good news that He is among us, aiding us in our walk of recovery, while we spread His graciousness of our saving to others.

Let us pray:
Dear Heavenly Father, thank you for loving me when I was still a sinner, Amen.

Verse 351

"Instead, let the Spirit renew your thoughts and atti-
tudes." (Ephesians 4:23)

Words for thought:

Let us think about this for a moment: when we were in our drunken stupor, day after day, we repeated to ourselves words of self-loathing and disgust. Our self-talk of, "I'm worthless, nobody cares, I hate myself, I hate you, you did this to offend me, I'm depressed, I'm angry, I'm ugly, I'm disgusting, I'll never stop drinking no matter what they say," kept us putting the bottle to our mouths as we tried to drown out the sound of our own voice. Our disease and Satan controlled our thoughts for many, many years, but God's voice was to be heard also, because He kept whispering in our ear, "There is hope, there is hope, there is hope." One day, His voice boomed over all the other noise and this day was our saving grace; it was our spiritual awakening, because from that day forward, we never had to put that bottle in our hands and then to our lips again. God tells us that we can be "tenderhearted and kind to each other, that we can forgive one another as long as we get rid of the bitterness, rage, anger, harsh words and slander, as well as all types of evil behavior" (Ephesians 4:31-32). See, there is a solution for us living one day at a time. We can choose that day to live without the insanity of the booze, and we can choose to travel the road of sobriety that God has given.

Let us pray:
Dear Heavenly Father, thank you for being my sovereign God, Amen.

Verse 352

"I love the Lord because He hears my voice and my prayer for mercy. Because He bends down to listen, I will pray as long as I have breath." (Psalm 116:1-2)

Words for thought:

The next twenty-four hours are the most important hours given to us. We have to make small beginnings on our road to recovery. At first, we may have a bad attitude as we adjust to living life sober, but if we "do" the work, our days will be filled with gladness and gratitude. Remember, we are seeking God so He may bring us to sanity and a soundness of mind. We do not have the ability to fight alcoholism alone, and that is why God tells us to humble ourselves under His mighty power, and give to Him all our cares and worries, because He cares for us. He promises to lift us up in honor at just the right time. So let us worship His name in glory for all He has done.

Let us pray:
Dear Heavenly Father, thank you for being the voice of truth, Amen.

Verse 353

"I listen carefully to what God the Lord is saying, for He speaks peace to His faithful people. But let them not return to their foolish ways." (Psalm 85:8)

Words for thought:

We are our own worst critic. We couldn't accept anything about ourselves, let alone any person, place, or thing. We set our morals on lower ground and we drove this behavior harder and harder with each drink. The more we drank, the darker we became. We lacked integrity, dignity, worthiness, and decency. Whatever our drug of choice, it became more important to us than family, friends, careers, and health. It robbed us of years of goodness on this earth. Once we were given this miracle of sobriety, we could look in hindsight and see we were not despicable people after all. We found a sense of a new happiness and new freedom. We felt we could live life sober and to its fullest on higher ground with God's commands. So let us enjoy this new season of life and do not try to understand everything. Always trust that God is good, just, and faithful in our exact time of need.

Let us pray:
Dear Heavenly Father, thank you that nothing is too big for you to handle, Amen.

Verse 354

"Keep watch and pray, so that you will not give into temptation. For the spirit is willing, but the body is weak." (Matthew 26:41)

Words for thought:

Our program is a gift and it started with God, and one alcoholic talking to another, and those two talking to a third, unbeknownst to them, at the time, our solution began. Our reward for twelve-step work is that we get to remain sober another day. On our daily adventure we get to take personal inventory (step ten), and when we are wrong, promptly admit it. By doing so, we are assured that resentments will not swell up in our souls. When we seek God in prayer and meditation in all we do, our spiritual practice gives us balance and open communication with Him at anytime, anywhere. While we are seeking His will for our lives, He gives us all power to carry it out. Thy will be done, not mine. Hallelujah!

Let us pray:
Dear Heavenly Father, thank you for allowing your word to be my source of hope, Amen.

Verse 355

"Commit your actions to the Lord, and your plans will succeed." (Proverbs 16:3)

Words for thought:

We must want to have God in our lives in all we do, and make Him come first above all things. Our struggles with alcoholism kept us in a small closet with no way out. Our illness allowed us to spend more time with evil than it did with good. So how do we open the door to freedom? We do it one day at a time. We do it by putting God first and not the bottle. We do it by sharing our experience with others who feel there is no hope. We do it by keeping our sobriety a priority. So let us ask ourselves: am I putting God and my program first?

Let us pray:
Dear Heavenly Father, thank you for using my past regrets and brokenness, and then turning them into something magnificent, Amen.

Verse 356

"He gives power to the weak and strength to the pow-
erless." (Isaiah 40:29)

Words for thought:

It's so wonderful how life can become beyond our wildest dreams. However, that can all change on any given day with a drink, a thought, an action, a reaction, a word, a phone call, a text, or an email. Life is so uncertain. However, what is certain is God's unchanging Word, love, and forgiveness. The Lord should always be our priority, because we have been redeemed.

Let us pray:
Dear Heavenly Father, thank you for allowing me this won-
derful life. A life I choose to live sober, Amen.

Verse 357

"God saved you by His grace when you believed. And you can't take credit for this; it is a gift from God. Salvation is not a reward for all the good things we have done, so none of us can boast about it." (Ephesians 2:8-9)

Words for thought:

I t is a gift when we are called by God to become sober. A gift sometimes only given once, because there is no guarantee if we take our own will back, that we will be offered God's saving again. The fact is some of us come into recovery and remain alcohol-free and continue to pass on the gospel of our program. Others test the waters to see if life drunk got any better, and discovered it hasn't, but are able to return to the rooms. Unfortunately, there are those we bury. They are the ones who just couldn't or wouldn't become honest enough to do the work. Although we do not sit in judgment of any "type" who suffers, we do stick with the winners in the program.

Let us pray:
Dear Heavenly Father, thank you for allowing me to overcome my alcoholism, and giving me the courage, strength, and wisdom to remain sober, one day at a time, Amen.

Verse 358

"But when you pray, go into your room, close the door and pray to your Father who is unseen. Then your Father, who sees what is done in secret, will reward you." (Matthew 6:6)

Words for thought

Prayer opens the door to God, and His Word tells us we can ask anything in His name, and if it is His will, He will do it. God saved us from death and darkness and showed us light and mercy. He saved us from our own prison of alcoholism. Let us run to Him with thanksgiving and praise.

Let us pray:
Dear Heavenly Father, thank you for my life today. Thank you for the people in my life. You have blessed me abundantly with family and friends, Amen.

Verse 359

Once we, too, were foolish and disobedient. We were misled and became slaves to many lusts and pleasures. Our lives were full of evil and envy, and we hated each other. But when God our Savior revealed His kindness and love, He saved us, not because of the righteous things we had done, but because of His mercy. He washed away our sins, giving us a new birth and a new life through the Holy Spirit. (Titus 3:3-5)

Words for thought:

When we are finally able to put our alcoholism into perspective, we learn it is a disease. This illness destroys us physically, mentally, emotionally, and spiritually. Once sober, we are able to take certain steps to abstain from alcohol one day at a time. We are then relieved from the bondage of self and become ready to fulfill the plans God has for us. Our Lord should receive our undivided attention, and we must pray on His will for our daily lives by staying focused on His commands. But remember, we must remain on guard for anything that will take us away from God, because evil lurks in the shadows, waiting to take us away from His grace, mercy, and wisdom.

Let us pray:
Dear Heavenly Father, thank you for giving me the strength to handle whatever may come my way today, Amen.

Verse 360

"For the Lord grants wisdom! From His mouth come knowledge and understanding. He grants a treasure of common sense to the honest. He is a shield to those who walk with integrity. He guards the paths of the just and protects those who are faithful to Him." (Proverbs 2:6-8)

Words for thought:

It used to be when we were alone and isolated we thought we were fine. We didn't need anybody because our best friend, alcohol, was all we wanted. Our minds became tortured by the feelings of uselessness, self-pity, hatred, and our number one offender: resentment. No matter how many hands family and friends reached out to us, we denied their help, and no matter how many times God prompted us, we couldn't or wouldn't listen. So we kept falling deeper and deeper to the bottom of our alcoholic hell, until we reached our end. See, liquor doesn't discriminate; it comes after us young, middle-aged, or old. After a while, we begin to see the results of sobriety, and we witness recovery can be similar or completely different, but we all can get there, no matter what, one day at a time. We remain sober with complete abstinence, fellowship, the twelve steps, working with another, and by God's grace.

Let us pray:
Dear Heavenly Father, thank you for corrected me when I am wrong and praising me when I do good, Amen.

Verse 361

"My Father taught me, take my words to heart. Follow my commands, and you will live." (Proverbs 4:4)

Words for thought:

O ur minds are so full of negativity and pride. Our minds are constantly tested by our everyday drinking. The enemy keeps infiltrating our thoughts, keeping us far from hearing the Word of God. We must remember the mind is Satan's playground, but the heart belongs to our loving God, and we are to guard it above all else, for it determines the course of our life (Proverbs 4:23). Our alcoholism results in spiritual battle. Our higher and lower power both want us; however, God wants us to live and Satan wants us to destroy. God intends to lift us up and show us love, forgiveness and mercy. He assures us there is nothing too big from which He cannot rescue us. Hallelujah!

Let us pray:
Dear Heavenly Father, thank you for making me see that my life is worth living, Amen.

Verse 362

"To everything there is a season, and a time to every purpose under heaven." (Ecclesiastes 3:1)

Words for thought:

We all have different seasons in our lifetime. We spent one of these seasons entirely drunk. It wasn't until we learned of the insanity of our disease that we could begin to heal. Our lesson along the way was to stop doing the same thing over and over again. Now we are on a journey of recovery, but we must always remember that passage never comes to an end, because if we think we've got it, then that will be the day we drink again. God has blessed us with another season, another way of life, a life to live sober. He has offered us a second chance to make amends and reunite with those alcohol stole from us: parents, siblings, children, friendships, careers. Let us take this task and glorify God and spread His good word to others who suffer the same malady of our disease, alcoholism.

Let us pray:
Dear Heavenly Father, thank you, for I truly felt my end was near, and you made it but a beginning, Amen.

Verse 363

*"He alone is your God, the only one who is worthy
of your praise, the one who has done these mighty
miracles that you have seen with your own eyes."
(Deuteronomy 10:21)*

Words for thought:

When we were so drunk and falling down, Satan loved us.
When we were in a drunken stupor, Satan loved us because
we only made wrong choices. When our speech was slurred and
we were unable to speak, Satan found comfort in this because
we could not speak God's Word. Up until the moment we surrendered our alcoholism to God, Satan knew we would do it his
way, because our choices were controlled by our sins. When
we put the drink down and began speaking God's truth, Satan
began to flee. When we choose God's will for our life, He helps
us fight the good fight against our sinful nature, and the great
news is we need only ask. Every morning, we ought to petition
Him to direct our thinking, and then be still, because He will
supply the grace for us to do His work. So today, let our eyes
be fixed on the Lord and allow His Holy Spirit to live in us and
through us.

Let us pray:

*Dear Heavenly Father, thank you for using me, even when I was
sinful, to do something great with my life, Amen.*

Verse 364

*"It is pleasant to see dreams come true, but fools refuse
to turn from evil to attain them." (Proverbs 13:19)*

Words for thought:

For those of us who indulged in our alcoholism every single day, know it is because we were focused only on self. We allowed our minds to rule our heart because we felt God was absent to us. God is full of love and we were full of fear, resentment, and hate, so how could we possibly give God's love to others when there was so much self-hatred? We would ponder and we would dwell on the wrong others did onto us, and in return, we carried guilt, shame, and remorse for what pain and agony we caused them. With all the anger, heartache, pity, and immorality that filled our hearts, it was impossible to find serenity. That is, until we became honest with ourselves and opened our hearts to God, our Father. Once we were willing, our hopes and dreams began to soar high, and maybe, for the first time, we began to believe what is written: "Come to me, all of you who are weary and carry heavy burdens, and I will give you rest. Take my yoke upon you. Let me teach you, because I am humble and gentle at heart, and you will find rest for your souls. For my yoke is easy to bear, and the burden I give you is light" (Matthew 11:28-30).

Let us pray:
Dear Heavenly Father, thank you for being my most high. Thank you for giving me the ability and wisdom to follow you through the rest of my days, Amen.

Verse 365

"Lord, sustain me as you promised, that I may live! Do not let my hope be crushed." (Psalm 119:116)

Words for thought:

A s addicted human beings, it is imperative we remember but for the grace of God go I. This glorious gift of sobriety we have been given gave us a new life to live. We learned to stay sober one day at a time and to accept life on God's terms. In return, He gives us fruits of the spirit to satisfy our soul of "love, joy, peace, patience, kindness, goodness, gentleness, faithfulness, and self-control" (Galatians 5:22-23). We no longer have to drink, because God promises to give us comfort in our darkest hour. His strength will hold us when we are weak. His Word is a lamp to guide our feet and a light for our path. He is our refuge and our shield; His Word is our only hope. God's love defends us against all evil. Hallelujah!

Let us pray:
Dear Heavenly Father, thank you for taking all my errors in life and turning them into my greatest strengths, Amen.

Verse 366

"And what do you benefit if you gain the whole world but lose your own soul? Is anything worth more than your soul?" (Mark 8:36-37)

Words for thought:

It is never too late to be saved from a drowning death of alcoholism. God is waiting, patiently, to give us the miracle of life. We no longer need quick fixes of alcohol, uppers, downers, shopping, binging, gambling, self-mutilation, sex, porn, and more to get us through our day. So let us take a look at what the common denominator is to all these obsessions. It is the compulsion: the irresistible urge to behave in a certain way, especially against one's conscious wishes. The insanity is we know these things only lead to death's door, but on our own will, we could not save ourselves. We needed the will of God. 1 John 2:15-16 plainly gives us the blueprint by which God wants us to live:

Do not love this world nor the things it offers you, for when you love the world, you do not have the love of the Father in you. For the world offers only craving for physical pleasure, a craving for everything we see, and pride in our achievements and possessions. These are not from our Father, but are from this world.

God is our brand-new beginning. He is the miracle through millions of others who share their experience. We all have a story to tell. A story of our hope, faith, and courage. We must allow our heart to long for God, and not the drink. Remember: only an open heart, willing mind, and rigorous honesty can heal us. God is calling, but are we listening?

Let us pray:

Dear Heavenly Father, on day 365 (January 12, 2018), I am concluding my final prayer of thanks. There is no coincidences in this world, only blessings. Today, by your grace, I am celebrating my third anniversary and on this day, my book has been completed for publication. I pray to share your word and wisdom with countless of others who suffer from this insidious disease of alcoholism. All the glory be to you, Lord, Amen.

CPSIA information can be obtained
at www.ICGtesting.com
Printed in the USA
BVHW04s0229200918
527999BV00006B/14/P